WAHIDA CLARK PRESENTS

CHRISTOPHER "DRUMMA BOY" GHOLSON

BEHIND THE HITS

WITH TAMIKO HOPE

Copyright © 2023 by Christopher "Drumma Boy" Gholson All rights reserved.

No part of this publication may be reproduced, stored in a retrieval system, or transmitted in any form or by any means, electronic, mechanical, photocopying, recording, scanning, or otherwise, without the prior written permission of the author.

Limit of Liability/Disclaimer of Warranty: This publication is designed to provide accurate and authoritative information in regard to the subject matter covered. It is sold with the understanding that neither the author nor the publisher is engaged in rendering legal, investment, accounting or other professional services. While the publisher and author have used their best efforts in preparing this book, they make no representations or warranties with respect to the accuracy or completeness of the contents of this book and specifically disclaim any implied warranties of merchantability or fitness for a particular purpose. No warranty may be created or extended by sales representatives or written sales materials. The advice and strategies contained herein may not be suitable for your situation. You should consult with a professional when appropriate. Neither the publisher nor the author shall be liable for any loss of profit or any other commercial damages, including but not limited to special, incidental, consequential, personal, or other damages.

BEHIND THE HITS
By Christopher "Drumma Boy" Gholson

1. Business & Music 2. Self-development 3. Music Production: Lifestyle– General

Hardcover ISBN: 978-1-957954-31-8
Paperback ISBN: ISBN: 978-1-957954-32-5
Ebook ISBN: 978-1-957954-33-2

Library of Congress Control Number: 2023902537

Cover Photo: Zach Wolfe
Back Cover Photo: Dominic Fondon
Exterior & Interior Design: MoneyGraphics LLC
Creative Design Team: Nuance Art LLC and MoneyGraphics LLC
Edited by Wahida Clark, Khloe Cain

Printed in the United States of America

Wahida Clark Presents Publishing
P99 Wall St #1521
New York, NY, 10005
1(866) 910-6920
www.wclarkpublishing.com

"Your joy is the greatest contribution you can make to life on the planet.

A heart at peace with its owner blesses everyone it touches."

- Drumma Boy

Photo by Dominic Fondon

This book is dedicated to my brother,
ENSAYNE WAYNE.

> *"GET TO SHAKING SOMETHING CUZ THAT'S WHAT DRUMMA PRODUCED IT FOR"*
> — DRAKE

> "Drumma Boy had that type of sound. It's like, that's why he going to be on all these big albums because the way his music sounded, it sounded like an industry standard sound."
> — ZAYTOVEN

> *"DRUMMA ON THE BEAT LEMME TAKE MY TIME"*
> — WALE

> "Drumma Boy had always maintained a certain level of authenticity within himself and that to me is valuable."
> — T.I.

> *"DRUMMA SQUAD BEHIND US MANE, THE TRILLEST THAT YOU FINNA SEEE"*
> — BUN B

> "You know I loved a lot of Drumma Boy beats coming up. He really got that Memphis sound. And that Memphis sound, like Three 6 Mafia and all that, that's really where a lot of the sound going on right now came from."
> — METRO BOOMIN

AYE YEAHHH BOY

Life Before Life..i
His-Story..iii
Parental Advisory..vii
Track 01: Tela "Tennessee"..01
Track 02: Yo Gotti "Life"..07
Track 03: Gangsta Boo "Sippin' & Spinning"......................................11
Track 04: Pastor Troy/D.S.G.B. "Off in Dis Game".............................15
Track 05: Boyz N da Hood "Trap N*ggas"...19
Track 06: Young Jeezy "Standing Ovation"...23
Track 07: Yo Gotti "That's What's Up (Intro)".....................................29
Track 08: Lil Scrappy "Like Me"..33
Track 09: Paul Wall "Gimme Dat"..37
Track 10: Young Jeezy "The Realist"..41
Track 11: Boyz N da Hood "Paper" ft. Rick Ross.................................45
Track 12: USDA/Young Jeezy "White Girl"...49
Track 13: Plies "Shawty" ft. T-Pain..53
Track 14: Yung Joc "Livin' the Life"..57
Track 15: Gorilla Zoe "Juice Box" ft. Yung Joc....................................61
Track 16: Playaz Circle "We Workin'"...65

LISTEN TO THIS

Track 17: DJ Drama "Gangsta Grillz" ft. Lil Jon..................69
Track 18: Scarface "Never"..................75
Track 19: Rick Ross "Hear I Am" ft. Nelly & Avery Storm..................79
Track 20: Rocko "Umma Do Me"..................83
Track 21: Young Jeezy "Put On" ft. Kanye West..................89
Track 22: T.I. "My Life Your Entertainment" ft. Usher..................93
Track 23: Plies "Plenty Money"..................97
Track 24: Gorilla Zoe "Lost" ft. Lil Wayne..................101
Track 25: Rick Ross "Face" ft. Trina..................105
Track 26: DJ Drama "Day Dreaming" ft. Akon, Snoop Dog, T.I...........109
Track 27: Gucci Mane "All About the Money" ft. Rick Ross..................113
Track 28: Gucci Mane "Watch Cost A Bentley"..................117
Track 29: Birdman "Money to Blow" ft. Drake and Lil Wayne..................121
Track 30: Gucci Mane "Coca Coca" ft. Rocko, OJ Da Juiceman, Waka Flocka Flame, Shawty Low, Yo Gotti and Nicki Minaj..................125
Track 31: Lil Jon "Throw It Up (Part 2) Remix..................129
Track 32: Usher "Stranger"..................133
Track 33: Gucci Mane "What's It Gonna Be"..................137
Track 34: Waka Flocka Flame "No Hands" ft. Roscoe Dash and Wale....141
Track 35: Young Buck *Back on My Buck Shit Vol 2: Change of Plans*..........145
Track 36: Musiq Soulchild "Waitingstill" with Jerry Wonda..................149
Track 37: Gorilla Zoe "King Kong"..................153

TRACK B*TCH

Track 38: DJ Drama "Oh My" ft. Fabolous, Rosco Dash, Wiz Khalifa...157
Track 39: Goapele "Right Here"..161
Track 40: Snoop Dogg & Wiz Khalifa "Smokin' On" ft. Juicy J.................165
Track 41: Young Jeezy "Lose My Mind" ft. Plies...169
Track 42: Gucci Mane "Thank You"..173
Track 43: 2 Chainz "Money Machine"..177
Track 44: Wiz Khalifa "Bluffin'" ft. Berner..181
Track 45: 2 Chainz "U Da Realest"..185
Track 46: Ledisi "Rock With You" ft. Jerry Wonda......................................189
Track 47: August Alsina "No Love" ft. Nicki Minaj (Remix)....................193
Track 48: Young Jeezy "Me Ok"..197
Track 49: Gucci Mane "I Think I Love Her" ft. Ester Dean.....................201
Track 50: Migos "Look at my Dab"..205
Track 51: Young Dolph "Both Ways"..209
Track 52: Yo Gotti "Imagine That"..213
Track 53: Gucci Mane "All My Children"...217
Track 54: Gucci Mane "Out The Zoo"..221
Track 55: Young Dolph "How I Feel" ft. Gucci Mane...............................225
Track 56: Young Dolph "While U Here"...229
Track 57: YoungBoy Never Broke Again "We Poppin'" ft. Birdman.......233
No Life Without Music..239
Thank You..241

Photo by The Speedy Butterfly

LIFE BEFORE LIFE

Coming into a world filled with black is the introduction of music to me. Science says that life begins at conception, which means there's life before life. I want to take a moment and ask you to cup your hands over your ears and close your eyes. Now, slowly say, "hello," three or four times. I'm sure that you've heard the sound of your voice but in a muffled tone. The recordings taken of babies around week 25 inside the womb reveal that about half of external noises are muted. That's what they hear. But in that warm, dark space— unable to see or touch the outside world— the most transparent sound they hear is the constant pounding of their mother's heart. Between conception and birth, the heart is said to beat approximately 54 million times. That's incredible to me. Although I didn't get the name Drumma Boy until I was in high school, when writing this book, I couldn't help but correlate that my fate had been set before I exited my mother's womb and arrived on planet earth. I'd like to think that every beat of her heart was like a drum's rhythm; I heard it and I felt it, which penetrated every vessel of my entire little body.

Her playing R&B from legends like Earth, Wind & Fire, the Temptations, Michael Jackson, Marvin Gaye, and combined with my dad playing the clarinet solidified the career path I've been on for over three decades. While my parents gave me the government name of Christopher James Gholson, I was Drumma Boy long before that. My mom said I kicked whenever I heard old school soul music, but I'd get real still whenever she played love ballads. Go figure. I'm still that same cool ass playa, too. When I was around six or seven, I started having these recurring dreams, like these déjà vu moments where I heard certain sounds before. I asked my mama what she thought that could mean, and she told me these stories about how she'd put her stomach up to the speakers in the house, and I would just go crazy kicking. That's when my eyes started opening up, and I realized that's where all these beats in my head were coming from; it all started when I was still baking in my mama's womb.

There's always been a rhythm in my head since before I got here. It would feel like a nightmare until I learned how to make beats. Then I was able to turn those nightmares into a positive reality. My older brother, Ensayne Wayne, introduced me to making beats and I instantly fell in love. It has nothing to do with fame; it's not something I do for money. I was born into this and embraced every moment of it. Being in the studio for the first time as a kid, I wanted it pitch-black, just like in the womb, that way I could tap into that familiar sound, feel of the music, and let it communicate to me. For me, it's always been about a vibe. The less visual noise you have, the more you can eliminate distractions and focus on the sound and be more creative musically. Think about legends like Stevie Wonder, Andrea Bocelli, and Ray Charles, arguably three of the greatest to do it. They were all naturally gifted and lost their sight as kids. Don't get me wrong. I'm sure none of these artists would prefer to be without sight, but I'm saying that it seems within the darkness, more attention is dedicated to the other senses to enhance creativity.

HIS-STORY

As most of y'all know, I'm from Memphis, born there, raised there, and super proud of my city and where I come from. Musically speaking, we have such a rich history in genres that span from gospel, rock & roll and country, to funk, soul, and R&B. I consider myself a serious student of music and as someone who believes that you should research, learn, and respect the ones that came before you. I feel compelled to give all of those who purchased this book a bit of a history lesson, specifically on my city.

You can't get to know me without knowing who and what I respect. I promise you, I'm a rare breed. I don't play about this business' forefathers, especially those that are a product of Memphis. I didn't want to write a book that was just about me and what I've done; I need y'all to know about who birthed the genius in me if you want to understand the man behind the hits. I've always been a mental subscriber of the philosophy that each one should teach one, so it's within that vein that I'm gonna take y'all to school. The folks I'm about to mention are just a small sample of what Memphis' soil has nurtured besides me.

We were blessed with Willie Mitchell, a trumpet player, producer, and arranger who ran the now infamous Royal Studios. Although Mr. Mitchell passed away in 2010, his legacy continues to breed excellence in my city. The Royal Studios was one of the recording facilities where the Bruno Mars' single "Uptown Funk" was recorded. That recording went on to win the Record of the Year Award at the 58th Grammy Awards. It marked the first time in the Grammy Awards history that a Memphis-made record received this honor. Mr. Mitchell's career spans six decades. He not only produced for Al Green, but he's been widely credited for launching Mr. Green's career. He worked with Ann Peebles, Otis Clay, Syl Johnson, Denise LaSalle, Rod Stewart, and John Mayer. Mr. Mitchell was also signed to the record label Hi Records as an artist himself in the 70s. Although born and raised in Covington, TN, Soul icon Isaac Hayes is a transplant and is part of the infamous "Memphis Sound" along with Johnnie Taylor, The Bar-Kays, and Booker T. Jones. He started his career as a young musician, songwriter, producer, and composer on Stax Records.

Second, only to Motown in sells and influence, Stax Records is one of the most essential soul music record labels of all time. In fifteen years, it placed more than 167 hit songs in the Top 100 on the Pop chart and 243 hits in the Top 100 R&B chart. Stax was also home to Otis Redding, whom Mr. Hayes used to work with as a keyboard sideman; his first job at the label. Mr. Redding's bio on the Memphis Music Hall of Fame's website opens with, *'He came to Memphis a valet and left a star.'* I think that perfectly reflects my city's spirit; a place where raw talent and opportunity meet. Although he died in a tragic plane crash at the age of twenty-six, thank God he blessed us with hits like "Sitting On the Dock of the Bay," which he recorded just three days before he died, and "Try A Little Tenderness," which was sampled on "Otis," Jay-Z's single featuring Kanye from *Watch the Throne*. And then there's Al Green, another product of the Stax mega-hit machine. Setting a new standard for soul music, Rev. Green became one of the top male soul singers globally and has gone on to pastor the Full Gospel Tabernacle Church located in Memphis.

Just as legendary as the artists themselves, there's Beale Street. It is to Memphis what Hollywood Boulevard is to Los Angeles. It's our walk of fame. Our southern Mecca for soul music, food, culture, and it is the heartbeat of the community. It's the mid-south cultural center; Black and white musicians were drawn to Memphis as a gathering place for social and musical activities. Beale Street gained fame during the Civil War as a social place for soldiers stationed in Memphis. The city has drawn gifted musicians from Mississippi, Alabama, and Arkansas. It has always been this thriving and special place where people could communicate their experiences and give their stories a voice and stage. It has also been established as a haven for Black people to celebrate their blackness. That pride shone through in notes, harmonies, melodies, beats, and chords.

Developed by Robertson Topp as a district for trade merchants due to its proximity to the Mississippi River Delta, Beale Street also has a rich legacy that highlights the practice of Black capitalism. It was one of the few places Black people could shop in the Jim Crow South. Robert Church— an entrepreneur, businessman, and landowner noted as the first Black southern millionaire, invested in Beale Street in the late 1800s. Due to segregation, he developed several upscale facilities for Blacks in Memphis including a recreational center, hotel, and concert hall.

Along with Josiah T. Settle, M.L. Clay, and T.H. Hayes, Robert Church established Memphis' first Black bank, Solvent Savings Bank, where he also served as founding president. He used the financial institution as a platform to help Blacks gain a better quality of life through access to loans for businesses and homes. I could go deeper, but I want to stay on topic for the book's purpose; however, when you get a chance, go check out Mr. Church's history and others. For him to have been moving like that during an era that was damn near an impossible scenario for a Black man will inspire you beyond belief. He was one of the pioneers who allowed Blacks to prosper at a time of great racial injustice.

That's why knowing your history is so important. How can you not go after your dreams after reading a story like that? How could you give up on yourself or let something hold you back, knowing what someone—who looked like you—endured back when your skin color was an automatic block? It's one of the reasons why I go so hard. If they could make their dreams happen and get to the money back then, I have zero excuses why I can't do the same thing now.

So, that's the cloth I'm cut from; from my immediate family members to the entrepreneurial pioneers of Memphis that came before me. This hustle mentality is built into my DNA. Knowing what Black folks accomplished in the early 1900s, owning establishments and businesses— which helped to make the music scene that much more successful— is an immediate source of motivation to me. Beale Street became home to barbecue, jazz musicians, and the "Memphis Blues" sound. This was where prominent figures such as: Memphis Minnie, Muddy Waters, B.B. King, Rosco Gordon, Bobby "Blue" Bland, Louis Armstrong, Albert King, and Rufus Thomas performed. All this Black musical excellence was created on Beale Street, giving it the electric energy that made it even possible for a young, white artist named Elvis to make history. Coming from Mississippi, he soaked up the soul and jazz culture of the OGs on Beale Street, hanging out at the clubs in the 1950s.

PARENTAL ADVISORY

I wasn't raised in a traditional household with both parents. My mother and father divorced right after I was born, so I shuffled back and forth between two houses as well as two different environments. I would look at other families that were all together and wish I could have that but that always showed respect for each other. They are complete opposites aside from the fact that they were both involved in and had a passion for creative arts. I inherited both of their love for music. I feel like I get my mom's hustle and my dad's work ethic. My mother was into the church, involved with the choir, but she also loved artists like Earth, Wind, & Fire, Frankie & Beverly, the Temptations, and more. She had a vast record collection that I was exposed to early on. She was always singing around the house, going to choir rehearsals, performing in the opera, or jamming to some oldies but goodies on the weekends while she would clean up the house. She would always tell me to have business together and the importance of money so I wouldn't need hers (Lol).

My mom, Billie Gale Baker, was born in Durham, North Carolina and raised by her parents stationed at the Army base during WWII. After tour of duty in the Army, her parents settled in Memphis, TN. Oldest of three siblings, Sara Marie, Leroy Jr., and Beverly, she had to develop leadership quickly as she attended Memphis City schools and graduated from Hamilton High in 1961. Billie went on to earn a Bachelor of Music Degree from Memphis State University at the time in 1965 and a Master of Science Degree in Operations Management from the University of Arkansas in 1981. Charter member of Epsilon Kappa Chapter of Delta Sigma Theta Sorority, she gained great relationships throughout the city of Memphis. As a vocalist, she performed with the Memphis Opera, University of Memphis performance of Porgy and Bess as well as a soloist for many church concerts and recitals. She met my father, Dr. James Gholson, Jr., taking my older brother, Wayne, to saxophone lessons at the University of Memphis.

My dad was the first Black principal clarinetist in the Memphis Symphony Orchestra for 39 years before retiring in May of 2012 after a career that spanned almost four decades. He also became the first Black professor at the Rudi E. Scheidt School of Music in 1972. As a member of the United States Navy Band, he appeared frequently as a soloist. Gholson studied clarinet in the Washington D.C. studio of Mr. Forrest, two blocks from the statue of General George H. Thomas. Gen. Thomas led the Union Army at the Battle of Nashville. He was the first among civil war generals to use African-American volunteers strategically in his battle plans. Overcoming many obstacles and circumstances, Gholson wasn't expected to make it out, let alone make history. Still, that underdog *'underestimate me, I'm gonna show you'* hunger is built into the Gholson's DNA. My father was born in Norfolk, Virginia, and grew up Hampton Virginia the same area featured in the movie Hidden Figures.

Since my dad came up during a time when desegregation was still a new way of life, he had to fight against all types of oppression, both literally and figuratively to succeed. What is a Black man from the hood in Virginia supposed to know about playing the clarinet, let alone attempt to be the first chair in the Memphis Symphony Orchestra? If he didn't teach me anything else, he taught me how to remain focused on a goal until that goal was realized. He also taught me that whatever you want to achieve, put your mind, talent, and attention to it, and you could make it happen. That's what he did to make history in Memphis. An environment of oppression serves as pressure to stay the course and become excellent in your field of service.

I remember being at my pop's house on the weekends and during the summer when I was fifteen-year-old, he'd wake me up every morning practicing the clarinet scales. He didn't give a damn that it was 5:30 A.M., and I was trying to sleep. And trust me when I say that nobody, I don't care how tired you might be, can sleep through someone playing a clarinet scale over and over and over again. My dad told me that any notable scientist, musician, athlete, etc. had to practice maintaining their skills, especially if they want to perform at their highest level. *'Being great requires discipline and a strong work ethic,'* he'd always remind me.

As an adult, I realize he did and said all that for reasons other than to get on my nerves. He started playing the clarinet around the age of seven. Having that wind

PARENTAL ADVISORY

instrument in his hands was as natural to him as brushing his teeth or taking a bath; he didn't even have to think about playing. He knew the life's lessons I'd learn from witnessing him habitually practicing and how that invaluable information would serve me later in my journey.

Steve Jobs once said, *'You can't connect the dots looking forward; you can only connect them looking backward. So, you have to trust that the dots will somehow connect in your future.'* That resonates with me now that I'm a grown man with a pretty successful career in music of my own. When I rewind time to when I was coming up, I learned that I had to study, respect the basics first, and understand the foundation of music. I'm sure you all are familiar with the saying that you can't know where you're going until you know where you've been. That's what Pops was demonstrating to me.

I was one of those precocious kids who wanted to just rip open the boxes of my toys and start assembling them without reading the instructions. That was my initial approach to music. I figured if I gotta do this thing, let me just pick up the instrument and start blowing and figure it out as I go. And that may work for some, but my pops wasn't having it. He nipped that shit in the bud immediately. He taught me that there were no shortcuts to excellence. You've got to familiarize yourself with the ABCs of whatever it is you want to pursue. He also showed me that you've got to go hard on days when you feel like it and on the ones you don't. There's no room for an off day when you're aiming for genius levels. Through demonstrated actions, I acquired the attitude that no matter how sweet you think you are, you gotta practice consistently and study your craft.

He exposed me to the importance of repetition, which produces muscle memory. He could play on autopilot if necessary; those notes were so ingrained in his brain that he could rise to any musical challenge and meet it. I also saw how passionate he was, which reflected his work ethic and character. I don't mean to sound redundant, but rather to stress the fact that my dad was the first Black man to disrupt the musical landscape of the Memphis Symphony Orchestra and infiltrate it by being the first chair. By hearing him rehearse every day as he did without fail, I soaked up the necessary ingredient for success, and that commitment is vital. It is the ultimate show of faith in yourself.

Music has made me a good listener. You must train yourself to discover how to make the sounds you want or recreate sounds in other songs you like. It's just like when you go out to eat with someone who's a true foodie. After they taste a dish they like, they've trained themselves to identify those flavors. They can make it at home and probably make it even better. You also must know when you're playing a note right or wrong. My dad was good at pointing out when I was doing something wrong but to always keep playing. Never stop when you make a mistake. You can practice all you want to, but if you're practicing wrong, all you're doing is strengthening your technique to play wrong. Changing the way you say something can change the way it's felt and the same goes for music. Got to learn the foundation of music first and create the emotion.

Music is like art to me. The beats allow me to dream up a story, paint what I want to see and feel, and the mood I want to convey. Music taught me how to establish a routine. If you look at any successful person or company, you will find that they've succeeded because they found a formula— a routine that worked for them, and they kept at it.

My first instrument was a little recorder that my dad gave me and taught me how to play when I was like three or four, and then by the time I was five or six, he put an E-flat clarinet in my hand, which I mastered quickly. I also got a toy piano that I used to bang on. When my dad realized I had some potential, he had a creative music teacher named Ms. Jones, who had me reading music drills and doing short technical études. Bobbi Jones, one of Isaac Hayes' musical mentors, also schooled me on the keys. By the time I was seven or eight, I could read sheet music, all the fundamentals that I use to this day. When I was eleven, my dad had this program that was like a space bar, and every time you read the notes, you'd have to press the space bar to make a beat. It got so repetitious that I just started making beats on the space bar, not fully aware that I was learning the fundamentals of production.

As a result of all that training, I became a musician first and a producer second, which has made all the difference in my career. By him educating me on how to play several instruments, he allowed me to learn invaluable skills to create streams of income for myself outside of just making beats. Education and dedication was what I learned from my dad. He stayed in Orange Mound, which is located on the southeast side of Memphis. It was the first Black neighborhood in the states to be built by Black folks.

PARENTAL ADVISORY

While he was this classical clarinetist, he was this cool, hip cat from a solid middle-class community that was still in the hood but believed in education. He was born and raised in the DMV area before coming to Memphis. Both of my fraternal grandparents were educators. My grandmother was a pianist and music teacher, who held advanced degrees from Virginia Union and Columbia. And according to my dad, he heard Chopin and Mozart while he was still in the womb, which was exactly how I felt that feeling and memory of life before life.

My grandfather, who met my grandma when he took piano lessons from her, was the principal of Fairmont Heights in Prince Georges County, MD, the county's first comprehensive high school for African-Americans. He also graduated from NYU and Hampton, paid for by the Old Dominion state in Virginia. At that time, in the 1930s and 1940s, Blacks couldn't attend graduate school in VA. So that's a big part of why my dad wasn't that supportive of my career in music without graduating college first.

When I was a kid, before I could go play outside or head over to the YMCA, summer camp, or just to shoot hoops, I had to do all my homework and study for whatever upcoming tests I had. It got to the point where I wanted to stop going over there. With him, it was like I had school before and after school. It was always work, work, and work. It was a lot of intense homeschooling, but of course I appreciate it now.

On the other hand, my mom, the one I credit for my business acumen, lived in an area called White Haven (or Black Haven). She was the more lenient one. I think she was relaxed with me because she wanted to compensate for the family being divided even though she and my pop's split was mutual. Or maybe she knew my dad had that drill sergeant role covered, and she wanted to make sure I enjoyed my childhood beyond just doing homework and practicing music. Either way, I started getting into trouble because I took advantage of her cutting me some slack from my dad's toughness.

There was gang activity happening around us. I started getting involved with the wrong crowd and getting into a little neighborhood trouble. Although I wasn't selling drugs or anything, it was enough to where my mom moved us to Cordova; a suburb outside of Memphis. It was some real-life Fresh Prince of Bel-Air shit. So, I go from the hood and saying things like, "you know what I'm saying, my nigga," to hearing people say, "Oh wow, yeah, totally dude." That experience totally changed my life.

Around this time, my older brother, Ensayne Wayne (R.I.P), was doing a lot of production work with Three 6 Mafia, Jazze Pha, Carlos Broady, 8 Ball and MJG, and Slice T. Ya'll may not have heard of some of those names, but Slice T is the one who gave everybody in Memphis a sound kit back in the 90s. He was the dude who would be like, *"I got some new snares in...I got some new kicks in."* He taught Jazze how to work the MPC, and Jazze's dad, James Alexander, was a member of the legendary group the BarKays, an influential soul group from Memphis. My brother learned how to play the piano growing up, so he played keys for a lot of people and he had me adding in drums. I could do it because of that space bar exercise my dad had me doing for all those years.

If any of you have seen Karate Kid, my story is similar. Just like in the movie when Mr. Miyagi had Daniel doing all those chores "wax on" and "wax off" instead of doing karate, there were many times I was questioning why my dad made me do all the boring stuff associated with playing instruments. I didn't care about reading music or learning notes or scales or any of that. But in reality, just like when Daniel discovered he was learning karate all along, I learned how to play at a higher level.

At this point, my drum patterns were pretty good, and I started feeling myself, especially at school. Everybody started calling me *"Cafeteria King"* because I would take a pencil and my knuckles and imitate drum sounds on the lunch table and also on my desk in the classroom. People freestyled to my improvised beats, and soon I got the reputation for always beating on something. That's how I ended up getting the name Drumma Boy. It was super cool to see people from a completely different demographic entertained by my music. It really changed my life. We were just having fun.

To be honest, those were the best days of my life because there were no expectations; it was just a bunch of kids with a lot of time and talent getting together, vibing out, creating, and feeding off each other's passion. I encourage emerging producers and artists to appreciate the ride to the top, embrace the struggles, and disappointments and don't rush the process. When you look back, you'll realize that in those times when you thought you were at your worst, you were growing and learning as well as developing your character to handle all the things that come along with success.

PARENTAL ADVISORY

You'll experience different trials as you move up, and each phase builds you up to pass the next test.

I remember the day I had a pivotal career moment. Unlike my former school, Cordova was like Beverly Hills 90210. It was teenagers pulling up in the parking lot in Benzes, BMWs, Range Rovers, and every other kind of luxury car you could name. Not their parent's car, but their cars. There were a few white boys that had American whips, new Impalas, and Mustangs, but they also had Pinewood systems with 15" and 17" speakers in the trunks. You could hear these guys coming hundreds of yards away. Of course, hearing all that bass awakened my senses, along with my hustler's mentality. I saw an opportunity to parlay my skill set with their love of banging music playing to announce their arrival.

So, I made "bass tapes" and started selling them to these guys at $100 a pop, which was the best free marketing strategy hands down because they wanted everybody to know they were up on all the new shit. There was this one dude in particular named Jimmy, who was my best customer. He would always come to school about 15 minutes late on purpose, bumping my bass tapes so the entire school could hear him arrive.

Of course, that made everybody be like, "Yo Jimmy, where did you get that tape from?" And he'd say, "Man, this kid named Drumma Boy."

That was my first taste of success. Ironically, being in Cordova put me in the perfect opportunities. It gave me an atmosphere of people who had the money to buy what I was hustling. It was a different kind of hustle because I wasn't hustling drugs. In the hood, my name started ringing from work I did with guys in Bolton, TN and Black Haven Zone BHZ. My mixes were doing so well on campus at University of Memphis; I started to expand my enterprise by going to the mall with my CDs and selling them there. I was thinking and doing everything I could to keep my new revenue stream going. By doing promotion with Pepper aka Mouth of The South and meeting people in the streets, I earned respect throughout the city. I kept hearing everybody talk about this rapper from Ridgecrest on the north side and ended up bumping into Yo Gotti at the Mall Of Memphis.

Photo by Zach Wolfe

Photo by: Dominic Fondon

TRACK 01

DATE October 8, 2002
ARTIST Tela
ALBUM *Double Dose*
PRODUCED "Tennessee," "Strive," and "Wangin"

"IF IT AIN'T BENEFICIAL, IT AIN'T NECESSARY."
— DRUMMA BOY

I spent most of my high school years playing varsity basketball and making beats in my bedroom just trying to get on. My mom got financed a Roland XP 50 when I was in the 9th grade and that is what I used to make beats. Throughout high school, I made enough money to eventually get a MPC 2000XL and pay Mom back for helping me out. By the time I got out of high school I had a resume going for myself. I mixed, produced, and rapped in a group called The Faculty out of Whitehaven aka Black Haven and also produced and rapped in a group out of Chapel Hill, TN called Treal. I was able to learn and perfect my craft, which I feel like prepared me for the big leagues. My older brother, Ensayne, was always in the studio making beats, playing keys, working with Three 6 Mafia, 8Ball & MJG, Tela, and more! He was a well-known barber at this shop called Dynasty One, which all the rappers and locals would come to get a haircut and the women would get their hair done. I started sweeping for him at the shop so I could meet people and let them hear my music. I've always been a fan of Scarface and Tela and those were two guys I wanted to work with. Tela's big single "Sho Nuff" was one of the biggest songs out of Memphis where he mentions Rochelle Stevens, "used to do nails for Rochelle tail." Memphis is known for the playa, boss like, pimp vibes so getting a placement on Tela was a producer's dream in 2002.

"Tennessee" was the first song I ever had on the radio and my first placement.

I first met Tela through my brother, Ensayne Wayne. He was my introduction to the Hip-Hop world in Memphis. When I was a kid, he listened to artists like Gangsta Pat, Playa Fly, 8Ball & MJG, Three 6 Mafia, [Kingpin] Skinny Pimp, and played drums in the church. Like all little brothers, I looked up to him and had the utmost respect for everything he did. I wanted to dress like him, walk like him, talk like him, basically be the younger version of him. Wayne was fourteen years older than me, so it was almost like he was a father figure, too. When I was coming up, I'd see him hanging out with people like Jazze Pha, who was around the same age, and I would be in awe every time I was in his presence like, "Damn, that's *my* older brother."

Wayne was the first person to take me to a professional studio. I was getting into fights when I was in middle school. Even though I was playing basketball at the time, carrying a clarinet around wasn't the coolest thing to do. I earned my respect to the point where people were like, "Alright, he might play that clarinet but you ain't gonna fuck with him. He fights back."

I was completely submerged in the orchestra world with my mom and dad, in addition to being in a new environment in the suburbs. Wayne wanted to introduce me to another creative outlet for my musical skills. I remember walking into the studio for the first time and seeing all the different color lights like this is where I see myself. I felt like I was in a spaceship. I put in a lot of work cooking up beats every day for 5 years straight to the point I knew I was good at what I did.

I remember my brother calling me one day saying, "I got a play for you." Of course, I was down for whatever he had on the plate. He said to come down to House of Blues studio. Little did I know, the one call would change the course of my life. When I walked in, it was pitch-black except for these different color lights. Green. Red. Blue. They twinkled brightly, reminding me of the first studio I had been to. There were all these classic photos and memorabilia of artists like Issac Hayes, Aretha Franklin, and other famous artists that worked there before. The hallways were painted various themes of Indian and African figures and you could feel the spirits the minute you walked in.

There, I met Anzel "Redboy" Jennings, who was Tela's manager at the time. Everybody knew Redboy. Back then, he managed Bun B and was the right-hand man of

TRACK 01: TELA

J. Prince. Not only was he in the room, but so was Rodney Jerkins, Jazze Pha, and Slice T. Each of them was playing beats for Tela.

You gotta think, this was the early 2000s, and Rodney had produced hits for Destiny's Child, TLC, NSYNC, Brandy, Michael Jackson, Toni Braxton, and Britney Spears. He was one of the top beatmakers in the industry at the time. Jazze Pha was coming off the success of Ludacris' "Area Code" and Field Mob's "Sick Of Being Lonely."

My mind was going ham. I was young, hungry, and wanted to soak up as much game as possible. I sat there quietly, observing, and listening, but I was also prepared. I was only in the room really because my brother felt like I was ready and he asked, "where them beats at mane?"

Heart pounding and nervous but excited at the same time, I played about ten of my favorite tracks for Redboy and the whole room. Everybody was silent with that shocked look on their faces. Imagine all the legends listening to me, pretty much a nobody, but giving me my respect like, "ok ok lil bra." By the time I stopped playing beats, Redboy had selected five beats for Tela to choose from and listen to for possible placement on the album.

The next day, they called me to come back to House of Blues, where I had to play my beats for Tela directly. Again, anxious and excited, I played my tracks and watched as he selected three. Slice T was recording a lot of that album and one of the tracks he said we should pull up. That year we had just gotten the Tennessee Titans and I was like, "we need a theme song the team and our state." I ended up writing and recording the hook for "Tennessee" and talking on the intro. When I came out of the booth, everybody was impressed. I had earned my first major label placement and their respect. I was even paid $2,500 per track because that was my brother's price for his beats. He was already on the album with two placements and also established in the city with credibility, so they gave me the same rate for my tracks which totaled $7,500. When I got my check at 19, I didn't even have a bank account but quickly got one opened shortly after.

In the summer of 2002, I was getting ready to start my second year of college. Driving through the town in my brand-new Chevy Impala, I was blasting Luda's "Move Bitch" from my new stereo system. My phone was ringing off the hook as I rode around. You have to keep in mind, this was back when texting wasn't that popular because it took forever and cost money. So, I'm riding around, listening to the radio when finally I pick up the phone. The person on the line was telling me to turn to K97. Hanging up from them, another call came in, and that person was telling me the same thing. So, I turned to K97, and my entire world changed. *My* song was on the radio. The same song I had recorded a few years back with Tela was now on one of the major Hip-Hop stations. If I wasn't convinced then that this was meant for me, I knew when some of my homegirls called me. When the girls start blowing you up, you know it's real.

My homeboys was hitting me up too congratulating me like, keep going bro don't stop. I was relieved just as much as I was excited because I had been talking about the song for so long, and they were anticipating the project. My friends had seen pictures of me in the studio with Tela, which at that age and time in Memphis was a big deal. It was then that I knew production was something I wanted to do professionally. That one studio session was the beginning of my unification process throughout Memphis, starting with connecting Yo Gotti with Tela, Gangsta Boo, Haystak, Criminal Mane, and Slice T's lil brother Maru.

Double Dose album by rapper Tela through Rap-a-Lot Records, peaked at #116 on the *Billboard* 200 chart and #18 on the Top R&B/Hip-Hop Albums.

D-BOY TALK

SURROUND YOURSELF WITH OTHER CREATIVE INDIVIDUALS WHO HAVE A DEEP DESIRE TO WIN AND WORK TOWARDS BEING GREAT. IF YOU'RE AROUND NINE LAZY, UNINSPIRED, BROKE, PETTY, COMPLAINING, NEGATIVE PEOPLE, YOU WILL BE THE TENTH. ALWAYS REMEMBER THAT YOU'LL BECOME JUST LIKE THE PEOPLE YOU SPEND THE MOST TIME WITH; INVEST YOUR MOST PRECIOUS ASSET IN SURROUNDING YOURSELF WITH WINNERS.

TRACK 02

DATE May 13, 2003
ARTIST Yo Gotti
ALBUM *Life*
PRODUCED "Life," "On Da Grind," "U Understand," and "Shake It"

> *"I BET MY LAST ON ME. I ONLY WORK WITH ARTISTS THAT'S WILLING TO DO THE SAME FOR THEMSELVES."*
> *- DRUMMA BOY*

If you ain't all in on yourself, why would I be? Always remember you get out what you put in! Making sacrifices early on to be in the right place at the right time was something I got a kick out of. When you have a window of opportunity, that's when you start going in even harder because it's always easier to set up the next play. After the *Double Dose* album, I immediately put together another beat CD promoting my music throughout the area. Even though I had this big radio hit and had done records with a major artist, I was still driving to all the local malls, high schools, nail salons, barbershops, skating rinks; basically, any and everywhere young people congregated to promote my bass tapes and beats.

Having production credit with Tela and a single on the radio was great and all, but I knew that current success wouldn't sustain me if I didn't hustle to keep my name circulating in the streets. The importance of relationships became my goal of being connected to the artists, managers, promoters, DJs, and executives. My strategy was simple. I decided I would make up in numbers what I lacked in production credits. The more people who saw me, heard my name, and heard my music put me in a position to be heard and gain more respect.

Having the "Tennessee" record on the radio everyday did help me gain city notoriety and got people around town even more familiar with my work. I think it also helped my name become more credible and applied pressure to anyone wanting to work with me. People were like, "not only is he a producer but he's an artist as well." Yo Gotti's buzz was already crazy before we worked and I wanted to make sure I had something on his next solo album. Ironically, during one of my mall runs, I bumped into Yo Gotti again. That's how small Memphis was tho you could bump into people, especially in the music industry, pretty much anywhere. He said he was working on his *Life* album and needed more beats. We exchanged numbers again cuz he changes number like every week lol and setup some time to get in.

The second time we worked in was this studio called Phatidef, which was Nick Scarfo's studio. Nick Scarfo born Nicholas Jackson, was the founder of Prophet Entertainment (aka Prophet Posse), the founding home of Three 6 Mafia, Killa Klan Kaze and Phatidef Music. I ended up doing four songs on his major-label debut album *Life*, under Inevitable Entertainment and TVT Records producing "Life," "On Da Grind," "U Understand," and "Shake It". My brother also produced 4 songs and my producers under Drum Squad, Swizzo, also produced 4 songs on the *Life* album. My production team basically executive produced that album.

At this time in Trap music history you really had to be who you said you were and really about the life you rapped about and Yo Gotti was that; a legit dope boy and a real hustler. If I ever needed anything in any city, he'd make it happen. One time, I was headed to Chicago and Yo called me about some money that he owed me and wanted me to come to pick it up before I left. I headed to Ridgecrest from Cordova which was about 15 minutes away and we linked up. Not only did he pay me my money, but he also added a little extra and gave me a an ounce of weed to smoke for the trip. Gotti was that type of dude. He's always been cool and making sure everybody was straight. He was very supportive of my brother, our team, and me. It's crazy to think back to how much work we did together over the years; we came up together career wise and established a working relationship.

I was struggling in school around this time because I was barely going to class. Instead, I was spending most of my time in the studio. My goal was to make my name as big as possible before telling my dad, I was Drumma Boy. I wanted to be famous enough, so if I wanted to stop my education, I could without him flipping out. I knew he wouldn't understand my plan, and I knew he wouldn't respect me having only a few production credits on a few local artists' albums. I can see his side now. He and my mom had invested a lot of time and money into getting me to where I was up to that point. Therefore, anything outside of me securing a good job with benefits was nonsense. While my mother supported my music career, she also wanted me to be financially stable even though she knew what I was aiming for and working hard for. I'm grateful that she encouraged me to be persistent. I don't think she would've felt that way had she not seen how hard I was consistently grinding.

D-BOY TALK

WHEREVER YOU ARE, KNOW THE CODE. LEARN STUDIO ETIQUETTE, AND YOU DO THAT BY OBSERVING. IF YOU AREN'T ABLE TO GET IN A STUDIO, THERE ARE TONS OF YOUTUBE VIDEOS OUT WHERE YOU CAN WATCH AND STUDY THE DIFFERENT ROLES PEOPLE PLAY. IT'S NO EXCUSE NOT TO KNOW ANYMORE. TOO MANY RESOURCES OUT THERE. IF THIS IS THE BUSINESS THAT YOU SAY YOU WANT TO BE IN, GET FAMILIAR WITH EVERY ASPECT OF IT.

Photo by Thomas Jacobi

TRACK 03

DATE September 23, 2003
ARTIST Gangsta Boo
ALBUM *Enquiring Minds II - The Soap Opera*
PRODUCED "Sippin' & Spinning" and "City Streets"

> "YOUR BIGGEST MISTAKES HAPPEN
> WHEN YOU SECOND GUESS YOURSELF."
> - DRUMMA BOY

Gangsta Boo was amazing to work with on Tela's *Double Dose* album, and we became good friends. As soon as people got more familiar with the work I had in circulation on the radio, everybody in the city started reaching out, including Gangsta Boo. She was one of the hottest female rappers that I knew about outside of Queen Latifah, Eve, Mia X, and Lady of Rage. She wanted me to come to Atlanta to do some beats for her next album that Jacob York was the executive behind. Boo was the first rapper from Memphis I saw that spent a lot of time in Atlanta. She was cool with everybody including: Natina of the group Blaque, Cee-Lo, Goodie Mob, Outkast, Pastor Troy, and more! I was traveling back and forth between Atlanta and Memphis when she hit me up, saying, "I'm in Atlanta and need to buy some beats for a project I'm working on, let's connect." When I arrived in Atlanta, she invited me over to Natina's house off Panola Rd. I'll never forget how nice Natina was and she even made steak and eggs with toast that had Welch's grape jam on it and a cup of orange juice. After we ate we went to Boo's homeboy, Rio's, house and there was a full production studio in his basement. It was there where I worked and made the beats for Boo's album. We came up with two concepts: "Sippin & Spinning," where I sampled her voice and turned it into the hook and a record called "City Streets." She paid me for the two beats, and that money allowed me to stay in Atlanta for a few weeks, so I could network and keep making plays for more placements.

While I was in town, she plugged me in with different people and introduced me to DJs and artists looking for beats. She was really solid from the beginning, and I can think back on other opportunities she would give me on the strength of our relationship, which was instrumental at the start of my career. People always wonder where my loyalty to Boo comes from, and that is where. She plugged me when she was on and popping, and I never forget the people who were there for me from the beginning. Boo was like the sister I never had and always showed love. When she got her own apartment in Alpharetta, I would sleep on the couch often so I wouldn't have to get a room and make beats in her kitchen. Anytime we had ideas ready to drop and record, we would go over to Rio's house and record. During one of the first sessions we had, she paid for the studio time, got everything set up, and was excited to record. Well, instead of recording as we had planned, I spent the entire eight-hour block tracking out the beat and laying each track out sound for sound. This was my first time doing this during studio time, and it was crazy because it took the whole night to do it, and man, she was pissed. She was like "Damn man, I ain't even get to record." I can still hear the heat in her voice and see her face all scrunched up. "You've got to get on your shit, man. Makes no sense for you to take damn near all day dropping a beat. This shit ain't cool."

Coming from a family that doesn't believe in excuses and strives for excellence, I was devastated. I felt like I had just taken someone's money and burned it. I had always prided myself on professionalism and doing what I needed to do in a timely manner. I kept thinking, how are you going to call yourself a professional and not know your equipment? Or how to operate it? That's like a doctor operating on you, and he's not sure what instruments he needs to perform the surgery. You're not going to feel comfortable on his operating table. You've got to learn how to use your tools. Needless to say, it made me learn my equipment and machinery. I went back the next day, and I tracked the second beat out in thirty minutes. Talk about being happy, proud, and relieved. Boo was like, "Man, this mo' like it!" We finally finished both records that evening. Using that moment as a lesson in preparedness, I familiarized myself with all aspects of the studio. That session with Gangsta Boo became a truly defining moment in my career. Especially seeing how fast and swift she was with writing her verses and recording them. Boo was a seasoned vet and knew exactly what she wanted every time we worked together.

TRACK 03: GANGSTA BOO

Enquiring Minds II: The Soap Opera is the third and final solo studio album by rapper Gangsta Boo. It was released on September 23, 2003, via Yorktown Records. The album served as a sequel to her 1998 album *Enquiring Minds*.

D-BOY TALK

IT'S OK TO MAKE A MISTAKE, BUT YOU HAVE TO IMMEDIATELY OWN UP TO IT AND COURSE CORRECT AS FAST AS POSSIBLE. WHAT YOU DON'T WANT IS TO GAIN A REPUTATION FOR BEING UNPROFESSIONAL AND PROBLEMATIC. NIP THE BULLSHIT IN THE BUD, APOLOGIZE IF YOU NEED TO, LEARN THE LESSON, DO BETTER THE NEXT TIME, AND KEEP MOVING FORWARD.

Photo by Karetova

TRACK 04

DATE December 16, 2003
ARTIST Pastor Troy/D.S.G.B.
ALBUM Til' Death Do Us Part
PRODUCED "Off In Dis Game" and "Make 'Em Get That Money Right"

*"EVERYBODY WANTS TO GET LIKE YOU,
BUT NOBODY WANTS TO PUT IN THE WORK."*
-DRUMMA BOY

Driving from Atlanta back to Memphis had become a regular occurrence at this point in my life. The thing about being in Atlanta at this time was that a lot of opportunity was available in the music industry. There was just this unique, crazy energy in the air and so many different people to work with in rap, Hip-Hop and R&B. It was heaven for a producer like me who had a lot of beats and could cook up on the spot. During one of those drives, I received a call from Pastor Troy out of the blue. The first words out of his mouth were, "Man if I rap on another one of your beats without meeting you, we're gonna fight. I've been hearing about you, and I need some new heat." I sold beats to different clients in Chicago, Florida, and North Carolina and ironically, Troy did a feature for each client and rapped on one of my tracks. I was just in Atlanta four months prior making tracks for Gangsta Boo so I told him I could come work whenever he was ready for me.

Pastor Troy's music was always another version of crunk to me. He always had my respect, especially how he repped Georgia. His praise of my work was definitely a solid stamp, proving that my name was gaining even more respect in the streets. He arranged some studio time for the following week, which would give me enough time to prepare and study his albums beyond singles released. Work was always the priority, but any chance I had at getting back to Atlanta, I took it. When I finally pulled up on Troy at his studio, he gave me eight-thousand dollars on sight for two beats, which set my new rate. It made me move differently and gave me a different perspective on what hard work and determination could do for you. Your price can sometimes separate who is really serious about their craft. If you are willing to spend x-amount of dollars on yourself, that means you understand and see what you are about to make for yourself. I tracked out both beats he wanted on my Pro-Tools MBox and laptop in the Motel 6 I was staying at right around the corner from Troy's studio. I couldn't even sync each sound as I tracked out the beats, so I just lined up each sound one by one and made it happen.

When the D.S.G.B. album finally dropped the track "Make 'Em Get That Money Right," became one of the biggest anthems in the strip club. There I was, twenty years old and not even legally able to get inside of the strip clubs, and my record was going stupid. Not old enough to experience what people were telling me about, I didn't even trip. My name was popping in the city, and that's what meant more to me. As an up-and-coming producer, this was the kind of opportunity that set the trajectory for a successful career. I kept hearing, "Your name ringing, you got the juice." I felt how powerful one thing could be and the impact it had on making more people want to work with me.

It was then that the calls started coming in from everybody. Big Cat Records, who had signed Gucci, Block ENT, who had Boyz N Da Hood—even Noonie of Noontime Entertainment who had Ciara, Jazze Pha, Polow, Johntà Austin, Jody Breeze, and many more artists at the time. Each day I would make more music and stack up inventory daily to be prepared for any presented opportunities. This was the first time I understood that people were rocking with my movement and saw that I could deliver. Being prepared when an opportunity presents itself is one of the keys to success.

> **D.S.G.B. (Down South Georgia Boys) was a hardcore gangsta rap group launched by Pastor Troy, and included Lil Pete aka Peter The Disciple, Pin Head The Hellraiser and Black Out.**

TRACK 04: PASTOR TROY/D.S.G.B.

D-BOY TALK

PUT YOURSELF IN AN ENVIRONMENT THAT KEEPS YOU INSPIRED. CREATE YOUR OWN ALTERNATE WORLD IF YOU HAVE TO. TAPE WORDS UP ON YOUR WALL THAT MAKE YOU WANT TO GET OUT OF BED EVERY MORNING AND GO GET IT. LISTEN TO PODCASTS THAT GIVE FREE GAME LIKE GARY VEE'S AUDIO EXPERIENCE OR PUT ON AN AUDIOBOOK WHILE YOU'RE IN THE CAR, ON THE BUS/TRAIN, OR AT THE GYM. IF YOU STAY FUELED UP BY PUTTING POSITIVE MESSAGES INTO YOUR HEAD, IT WON'T LEAVE MUCH ROOM FOR ANY BULLSHIT.

Photo by Tony Tyus

TRACK 05

DATE June 21, 2005
ARTIST Boyz N Da Hood
ALBUM *Boyz N Da Hood*
PRODUCED "Trap Niggas" and "Look"

> "CHEMISTRY COMES WITH NO INSTRUCTIONS; IT DOESN'T HAVE A MANUAL. IT JUST FLOWS."
> - DRUMMA BOY

Coming off an incredible club run in 2004 with Pastor Troy's strip club anthem took my name to new heights. I turned twenty-one the summer of 2004 and finally experienced the strip clubs that my music had been rocking in for a while. It was crazy to me how many strippers would request my songs to be played on their sets. Once they started meeting me and found out I was the producer, they would give me tips on what rappers I should work with and who had money and didn't. I remember one girl telling me about Jeezy and said I should work with him. Once the tips started turning into placements, I would go back to the strip clubs and tip the girls to show my appreciation.

My manager, Squeak, was managing Jody Breeze at the time; one of the members of Boyz N Da Hood. So, naturally he approached me about us collaborating on some songs. But the funny thing was, we could never connect because he was busy as hell, busier than me, and that's almost impossible. One day, Squeak told me to come by Jody's video shoot for "Stay Fresh," produced by Jazze Pha. Some of everybody was there, and it was a good time to just get familiar with everybody on the team. That opportunity led to Jody saying to me, "Let's get in the studio tomorrow." The next day at Sho' Nuff studios, we did a song called "Stackin Paper" featuring him and Slim Thug. Squeak said he had Jeezy coming through for a second. When Jeezy arrived, we did a record called "Get Ya Gangsta On" and "Trap Niggas," where Jeezy and Jody were going back and forth on the verses. After doing those records, I could see that Jeezy was transitioning from being in a group to doing more solo stuff. We did a record called "Ya Dig," and I knew Jeezy was a star from hearing him on these records. His energy and delivery always made you knock your head, and the punchlines made you smile. I credit his engineer, Nico, as one of the people that helped Jeezy discover his sound. Jody gave a player/hustler vibe while Jeezy hit you with the voice of the streets.

Besides Jody and Jeezy, there were two other members in the group, Big Duke and Gee. They were signed to Block of Block ENT, a music exec from the east side of Atlanta. Block was a street dude that got into the business because he was a natural at putting plays together and recognizing talent. He also had a business relationship with Diddy. Together, they formed Bad Boy South with Block heading it up and holding down Atlanta. When Squeak told me Diddy's favorite record on the album was "Look," I felt closer to getting a gold or platinum plaque. When the album dropped and the Boyz N Da Hood tour was set up, I attended the show in Memphis and Atlanta. Jody Breeze had the girls and the other artists brought out the streets. Jeezy was already on tour before Boyz N Da Hood, so he might not make the show if the dates conflicted in some cities. The Memphis show Jeezy was unable to make, but the place was still packed, and Jody Breeze, Big Ghee, and Big Duke held it down. It was dope being able to connect my city with different acts I was producing. My nephews, nieces, and friends always came out with us to celebrate the rise of my career and continued success.

Block first started reaching out to me through Squeak, and he cut a check in advance. Block would always pay upfront cuz he never wanted us to have to wait on the label. He made sure I was paid and also made sure I was on every project released that he was a part of. I remember meeting Young Joc and Gorilla Zoe at Block's studio off Memorial Drive, where we would eventually work together. Block was the street exec before the Street Execs. Looking back, I think he respected my independent mindset and grind; he related to that and wanted to make sure I was straight, so I could keep hustling.

My career started to resemble a puzzle. All the pieces of hard work over the years were coming together and fitting into place. The Pastor Troy record was the one that put me on the map in Atlanta, and now I had Block ENT reaching out. He paid me

TRACK 05: BOYZ N DA HOOD

five-thousand dollars a track, which allowed me to set another increase in my rate. I had a bet with my father that I would show him one-hundred-thousand dollars in my bank account within a year after getting kicked out of the University of Memphis due to nonattendance, and time was ticking!

> *Boyz N Da Hood* peaked at #5 on the US *Billboard 200* and hit #1 on both Top Rap Albums and Top R&B/Hip-Hop Albums.

D-BOY TALK

Run your career like the enterprise it is. I've been able to do transparent business by putting my team in place early. I secured a reputable attorney first because I needed to make sure the contracts I signed were above board and fair. Next, was getting an accountant to make sure I paid Sam's begging ass and, a little later, a publicist to amplify what I was doing. I continue to add to my team as I grow, like hiring a videographer and photographer to capture my active schedule.

Photo by Robert Hector

TRACK 06

DATE July 26, 2005
ARTIST Young Jeezy
ALBUM *Let's Get It: Thug Motivation 101*
PRODUCED "Standing Ovation"

"NO POINT IN HAVING THE PLUG IF YOU NEVER PLUG IN."
- DRUMMA BOY

One month later, Young Jeezy dropped his solo album! When the project was leaked a couple of weeks early, everyone thought it would hurt the album's sales. Luckily, it made the project even bigger, being one of the *most* talked about projects in the streets and clubs at the time. Back then, especially the clubs, was where all the hot artists were, particularly strip clubs. So that was the place to be if you were a producer wanting to hustle up on some work. I was fifteen days away from turning twenty-two, and all the biggest promoters in the city had me lined up to host or do a walk-thru in Memphis, Atlanta, and New York. My first publishing deal was on the table for one-hundred-and-fifty-thousand dollars with Warner Chappell, which allowed me to officially win the bet I had with my father!

I remember bumping into Jeezy at the club. During this period in the city, you would always see him and BMF together. Jeezy was known for showing out of town guests the city of Atlanta and doing it big in the club. He had one-hundred niggas with him, iced up jewelry, Lambos, Ferraris, and plenty of money to blow. It was easy to see he was already a star. I was cool with a couple of cats from BMF, and I was also cool with a couple of Jeezy's homeboys. I knew Jeezy's brother, Clem, so whenever I'd see him out, I would always see Jeezy with him. But that relationship with Jeezy wasn't built overnight. Around 2005, I was this new young and hungry producer with a few bangers under my belt, so I was super confident in my abilities to deliver hits. However, at the end of the day, I was still new and earning my respect in Atlanta.

Even though we worked together a few times, I was still the new face that people had to get familiar with. 8Ball & MJG told me one time that they had to watch me for a few years before they would embrace me. People gotta know you're solid and not on the bullshit regardless of what you do. I must have gone up to Jeezy at least five or six times before my name and face card stuck.

'Aye mane, what's good bro, my name is Drumma Boy.'

'Aye mane, what's good bro, my name's Drumma Boy.'

'Aye mane, what's good bro, I'm Drumma Boy.'

This happened repeatedly until probably the seventh time he'd 'met' me. He finally was like, 'Man…damn bruh you be out here. You be out here working. Take my number.'

That's why you can't have any ego or chip on your shoulder or take things personally when you're trying to get on. I'm a go-getter, and I'm persistent, and I knew that if we locked in just once, he'd continue to work with me because I knew my sound would fit his style perfectly. And because I wasn't an amateur, I had a level of self-assuredness that didn't come across as being too anxious. My goal was for him to see me and know that I was serious. I remember Jeezy hitting my phone and telling me that "Get Ya Gangsta On" was going crazy in the streets. I felt like I had gained more trust from him when he saw the reactions to "Ya Dig," and "Trap Niggas" at his shows. He hit me up a few times for beats, and I ended up giving him a gang of beats to go through; there was one in particular that he liked, but I didn't know it at the time.

Six months had passed, and out of the blue, my phone started blowing up. Imagine seeing fifteen missed calls from Coach K and Jeezy. I knew it was about a beat, which meant it was about a check. When I called Jeezy back, he was like, 'Yo, I need this beat right here.' At the time, "Trap or Die" was out, and Jeezy was the city's biggest artist. As a producer, you want to be on his official debut album. I asked him to play the record he wanted, and as he played me the track, I realized that I had sold that beat a few weeks prior. I was sick! And he was like, 'What you mean you sold the beat?! I'm bout to get Jay-Z on this.'

TRACK 06: YOUNG JEEZY

I felt like he was popping game; I didn't think Jay-Z would get on "Standing Ovation" at that time. Jeezy continued to press me about this beat, asking who I sold it to and that he'd give them a hundred thousand for it. He offered to pay me double, even triple what I sold the beat for if I could get it back. At that point, there was no way I was going to tell him what I actually sold it for, which was five-thousand dollars. I told him I could remake the track if he'd just give me the acapella. He told me I'd be a bad muthafucka if I could top the original. And by the way, he wanted the beat ASAP.

At the time, I stayed in Stone Mountain and had to commute into the city. For those not familiar with the ATL's landscape, that's about a forty-minute drive each way. So, I got in my car and drove to Patchwerk to pick up the vocals because he didn't want to send it by email and take the chance of being hacked or the vocals being leaked. He was that serious about this record. After I picked up the vocals from Jeezy I drove back home and worked on the first version. I drove back to Patchwerk and I played the first version for him, and he was like, 'That ain't it.' So I drive BACK to Stone Mountain the second time and work on a second version because the album had to be turned in the next morning. I pull back up to Patchwerk and I played the second version, and he said, 'Aw man, that's close.' I was like man I got to make this album.

On the drive back home to Stone Mountain, I remember listening to the "Trap Or Die" mixtape over and over again, just studying the sound and his beat selections. The first thing that I noticed was that Jeezy loves horns because he had horns in every beat on the project. So that's the first sound I added when making the third version of Standing Ovation. Once I finished the beat I took it back to Patchwerk. I probably had less than a quarter tank of gas left and a few hundred dollars to my name. I played the third version for Jeezy and when he listened to it, he just laughed and let out that signature, "Ha Haaaaaaa."

It was the exact ad-lib you hear on his records today. He told me that since I came through for him like that and at the last minute, he had me forever, and that's how we created "Standing Ovation." This was incredibly huge in the streets because I did the 2nd track on the album that set the whole tone to Jeezy's career-establishing album; a song where he boldly proclaimed, "I am the trap." It was huge for me. This also marked the first record I ever had mixed by the legendary Leslie Braithwaite, who has mixed many big records for Cash Money, Lil Wayne, T.I., Destiny's Child,

Beyonce, TLC, Pharrell, and others. On top of all that, I earned my first platinum plaque which was a dope moment for me, Jeezy Coach K, Kinky B, Leslie, Shakir Stewart, Def Jam, my manager Squeak and everybody involved.

I felt like, ok, I'm officially in the game. This is the intro to an album, and that intro song went platinum. We got over a million downloads. That was crazy and huge to me because, again, it wasn't even a single on the album. "Standing Ovation" was also my first real claim to fame as far as being a part of that elusive platinum producer club that all beatmakers aim to be a member of. This song helped me close a publishing deal with Warner Chappell and pull through on the bet I made with my father. He found out I was kicked out of University of Memphis for 6 months due to un-attendance and we made a bet that if I didn't come up with 100k in my bank account in less than 12 months, that he would kick my ass and send me back to college. I remember going back to Memphis and showing him my bank statement and we've been best friends ever since. My dad wanted to know so bad what I was doing with my time and I was finally able to tell him, "I'm a platinum producer."

> *Let's Get It: Thug Motivation 101*, released on July 26, 2005, was Jeezy's first top-ten debut, debuting at #2 on the US Billboard 200. The album was certified platinum by RIAA on September 29, 2005. On July 2, 2020, RIAA certified *Thug Motivation 101* as 2x platinum.

D-BOY TALK

SPEAK POSITIVITY INTO YOUR LIFE EVERY DAY. INSTEAD OF HAVING AN OVERWHELMING BELIEF THAT THINGS WILL GO WRONG, FLIP IT AND HAVE AN OVERWHELMING BELIEF THAT EVERYTHING WILL GO RIGHT. YOUR THOUGHTS AND WORDS SHAPE YOUR FUTURE. JUST LIKE EATING JUNK FOOD WREAK HAVOC ON YOUR BODY, SPEAKING AND THINKING NEGATIVELY HAS THE SAME IMPACT ON YOUR LIFE. WHATEVER YOU CONSISTENTLY THINK ABOUT AND SAY WILL EVENTUALLY SHOW UP IN YOUR LIFE. CHOOSE CAREFULLY.

TRACK 07

DATE May 23, 2006
ARTIST Yo Gotti
ALBUM *Back 2 Da Basics*
PRODUCED "That's What's Up (Intro)" and "Warrior"

> "MUSIC HAS MADE ME A GOOD LISTENER. I'VE TRAINED MYSELF TO DISCOVER HOW TO MAKE THE SOUNDS I WANT OR RECREATE THE SOUNDS I LIKE IN OTHER SONGS."
> —DRUMMA BOY

After the success of Young Jeezy's *Thug Motivation 101* album, everyone was paying attention to my sound especially the dope boys. Jeezy would tell me often, "Imma fan of what you and Gotti on; y'all sound is crazy." Gotti and I teamed back upon his *Back 2 Da Basics* album, where we cranked out another smash called "That's What Up." This would be one of my first big singles I placed with him that went crazy in the streets and clubs. The other records we did on the *Life* album were just album tracks but "That's What Up" gained the streets' attention and blew up in the traps, clubs, and even a few radio stations. It helped me make a name for myself throughout the south and solidified me with the trap rappers like T.I., Jeezy, and Gucci Mane who later told me he related to the lyrics and the beat patterns coming out of Memphis. The song's popularity can also be credited to Gotti performing it at all his shows. When they're shouting you out on the records you produced at their shows and mentioning your name in interviews about their projects, it helps make the producer more than just some nameless person behind the beat.

I've always been one of those producers who prefer to have real studio sessions where we vibe, create, and establish a working relationship. Chemistry is something you can't make up, it just happens. The combinations of sounds, words, emotions, energy, and turning pain into fun are usually the recipe for a hit record. I consider myself a therapist and completely dive into the life of the client. I wanted to deliver something triumphant with the horns like "Standing Ovation" but with more of a club bounce. When he told me the album was gonna be called *Back 2 Da Basics*, I immediately started cooking up beats that felt like that title. Gotti did the rest, saluting and shouting everybody he did and didn't fuck with on the record. This record gave you insight on Gotti's hustle and his perspective on the streets coming from North Memphis.

To this day, I'm still putting in work with Gotti. He has always been an honorable guy and man of his word. It's one of the things I've respected about him since day one and over the years. Though he's an artist, he's also a stand-up businessman. If he says something, it happens. Everybody's experience with how they get paid will be different. Still, it's a big deal as a creative to get paid after you've rendered a service and sometimes before you even hit the studio. How I collected my coins always depended on who the artist was and how I knew them. If the connect was from a solid person that I knew and considered a friend, then my payment terms were flexible just because I knew relationships and backend would take me further. If it wasn't through a friend or family then I need a deposit or all my bread upfront. With Gotti, those types of problems never came up; he was always ready to pay when he pulled up. I never had to chase him down for my money or ask him repeatedly about when he was going to cut a check; he was on top of his shit. When you do good business, you earn repeat business, and that works both ways. As you'll notice throughout my discography, I've worked with and created smashes with a lot of the same people, and we're still working together. When you're able to deliver for people when they call your name, they will always be back.

TRACK 07: YO GOTTI

D-BOY TALK

NURTURE YOUR RELATIONSHIPS BECAUSE THEY CAN CARRY YOU FARTHER THAN TALENT WILL AND PUT YOU IN EXCLUSIVE ROOMS WITH PEOPLE WHO CAN OFFER YOU LIFE-CHANGING OPPORTUNITIES. A LOT OF THE PEOPLE I WORK WITH NOW, THOSE I ESTABLISHED RELATIONSHIPS WITH BY BEING GREAT AT WHAT I DO, AND DELIVERING RESULTS, AND DOING GOOD BUSINESS. PEOPLE MAY FORGET YOUR BEATS, BUT THEY'LL ALWAYS REMEMBER YOUR ENERGY AND CHARACTER. AND THE MUSIC INDUSTRY IS SMALL; IT'S LIKE A BIG HIGH SCHOOL. AT SOME POINT, YOU WILL CROSS PATHS AGAIN.

Photo by Dominic Fondon

TRACK 08

DATE December 5, 2006
ARTIST Lil Scrappy
ALBUM Bred to Die Born to Live
PRODUCED "Like Me"

"YOU GOTTA SPEAK IT INTO EXISTENCE AND STAY IN-TUNE WITH WHAT YOU BELIEVE IN AS YOU WORK TOWARDS YOUR VISION."
- DRUMMA BOY

I gained the relationship with Lil Scrappy in Memphis when he came to do a show with Lil Jon & Trillville. We dapped up everybody before and after their performances and always said we'd link up soon. While they were in town, we took them to a few studios they could be comfortable at and knocked out some work. Lil Scrappy was like the little neighborhood knucklehead, a real pit bull type. He could be cool, but you could also tell that he'd take down anything standing in his way to get what he wanted. He was strong-willed and had this unmatched aggressive energy, which you could understand after hearing him on "Knuck If You Buck" (2004) and "No Problem" (2004). That whole Trillville movement he was a part of was borderline crunk. It was like a division under Lil Jon and we could relate to it in Memphis. That's what we're known for is that Grit and Grind.

I bumped into Scrap again through my guy, OG Crip, who used to run S-Line Studio in Atlanta during that time. It was one of the main studios a lot of people used to work out of especially Warner Brother and Atlantic artists, and also a place where all the creatives linked up, talked shit, and handled business. I was in town working with a few independent artists and always checked in to see if I was needed. Even though I had Scrappy's email I always wanted to do sessions in person. Whenever we worked together, I always pulled up on him. On one of those occasions, I can remember pulling up to the studio, and Scrappy was finishing up the album. I was like, "Man, I got that work, mane. I need to be on the album I got some heat." I played about ten beats on the spot, and he picked out five. Out of those five, one ended up making the album.

We usually started sessions around 3 or 4 p.m. and went until 5 or 6 in the morning. The first song we recorded was "Like Me," and everybody loved the record so much it not only made the album but was the single. He also had established a cool relationship with my brother, Ensayne Wayne; my boy GK and Swizzo. Swizzo was one of the producers who signed to Drum Squad and did a few songs with Scrappy as well as my brother. We all would collaborate and make records for fun, just feeding off each other. It's crazy when you think back on how many records never came out. I was just happy I was able to deliver a song that helped push album sales.

Bred 2 Die • Born 2 Live released in 2006 and the album debuted at #24 on the *Billboard* 200 chart, which I think was impressive because of the pre-social media/digital age and the self-promo era. This was a time when street teams and album touring was heavy. Many acts come through Memphis for radio runs and shows and take advantage of our tri-state region touching southeast Tennessee, Arkansas, and Mississippi fans in one trip. Being able to introduce a new record in my hometown and deliver to the DJs solid material city to city and state to state is always an amazing feeling.

TRACK 08: LIL SCRAPPY

D-BOY TALK

EVERYBODY WANTS TO WORK WITH THE ARTISTS THAT ARE FAMOUS. BUT IF YOU MAKE THE PERSON NEXT TO YOU FAMOUS THEN EVERYBODY WILL WANT TO WORK WITH YOU.

TRACK 09

DATE April 3, 2007
ARTIST Paul Wall
ALBUM *Get Money, Stay True*
PRODUCED "Gimme Dat"

> "EVERY CITY I GO TO, I SET UP SHOP AND SERVE THE PEOPLE."
> -DRUMMA BOY

It's crazy how much respect I gained in Houston after the work I did with J Prince, Rap-A-Lot, and Tela. Redboy would always make sure things were great for my guests and me in Houston. We would hit all the known spots and show love to the DJs, bartenders, strippers, and artists. My older brother, Ensayne Wayne, was good friends with Scarface, and I ended up doing a song called "Never" for his *Made* album, which hadn't come out yet. I met Paul Wall in a few clubs and again in the mall with TV Johnny while I was out there. Having such a solid track record earned the likes of the top Houston artists like Bun B and Slim Thug. Once "Stacking Paper" dropped, a record I did for Jody Breeze featuring Slim Thug, people started hearing the versatility in the beats I produced.

You'll repeatedly hear me say this, but relationships are fundamental in this business, and it's essential to keep them intact. I reiterated that because when I think back, it's funny how my name was still being brought up in conversations through work I had done with Tela. Just goes to show that you should always put out the most quality work you can so it will stand the test of time. My beats are my resume, and as 3000 told us back in the day, *"you're only as good as your last hit."* As a result of all of that, Paul and I linked up for his third studio album. He had my number from when we met in the club and texted me like, "send me something for the album."

Even though we couldn't work together in the studio since we were headed back on the road, I emailed him five beats. He probably sent it back within twenty-four hours so I could get it mixed. When you hear Paul Wall rap, it just makes you smile for some reason. It's so jamming but at the same time fun, cool, and has that bounce. I couldn't stop saying, "I Need My Money, I Need My Cash." Of course, I had to add the classic "Aye yeaahhhh boyyyyys" to the intro because everybody know when I add those on a record it's serious.

One of my favorite memories from being out in Houston for the first time was getting a grill from TV Johnny, which was super cool. I had "Drumma Boy" spelled out in my grill with Drumma on the top and Boy on the bottom grill. I've always liked soaking up other people's culture and checking out what's hot in their city or country. When you're in Houston there are so many options of food that they offer from BBQ to soul food to fine dining. What I appreciated most about the people I met and worked with there was their hospitality. They were chill, laid back, and down to earth people. It was just how we'd treat them if they were in Memphis. They did the same by always looking out for me and showing love from day one and just being A-1 on making sure everything was solid. It was like being with extended family. It may not seem like a big deal, but I've been to a lot of places over the years and being around hospitable people that make you feel welcome ain't the norm.

Get Money, Stay True, **Paul Wall's third studio album, was released on April 3, 2007 and debuted at #8 on the US** *Billboard 200.* **The album also reached #1 Top Rap Albums and #2 Top R&B/Hip-Hop Albums charts.** *Get Money, Stay True* **was released by Swishahouse, Asylum Records and Atlantic Records.**

TRACK 09: PAUL WALL

D-BOY TALK

I HEARD A WISE MAN SAY TO NOT LET WHAT HAPPENS IN OTHER PEOPLES' LIVES, GOOD OR BAD, AFFECT YOURS. JUST BECAUSE SOMETHING WORKED OUT GREAT FOR SOMEBODY ELSE DOESN'T MEAN IT WILL TURN OUT LIKE THAT FOR YOU, AND JUST BECAUSE SOMEBODY ELSE FAILED AT SOMETHING YOU'RE DOING DOESN'T MEAN YOU'LL FAIL. YOU DON'T KNOW ALL THE FACTS OR FACTORS AS IT RELATES TO OTHER PEOPLE, SO DON'T LET "THEY" AND "THEM" SWAY YOU ON YOUR JOURNEY.

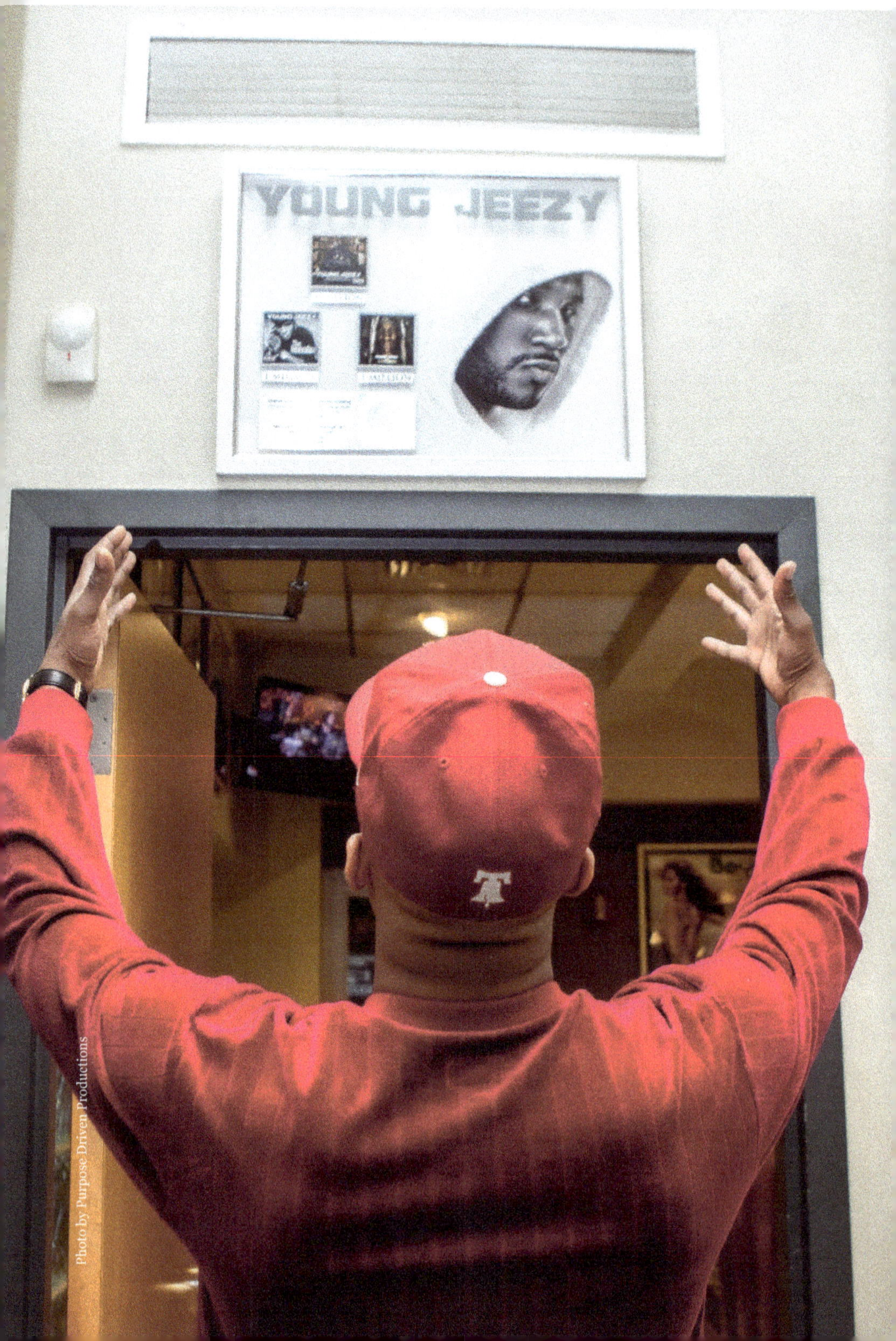

Photo by Purpose Driven Productions

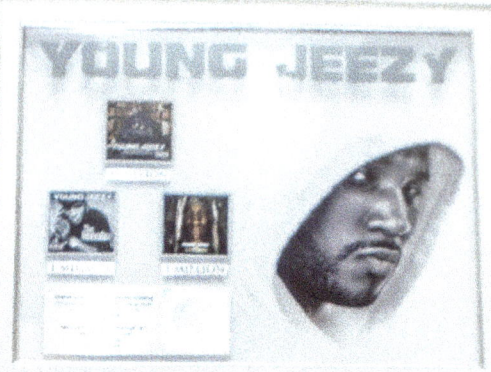

TRACK 10

DATE December 12, 2006
ARTIST Young Jeezy
ALBUM The Inspiration: Thug Motivation 102
PRODUCED "The Realist"

> *"IN STUDIO COOK UPS ARE LIKE A HOME COOKED MEAL. SENDING BEATS VIA EMAIL IS FAST FOOD."*
> — DRUMMA BOY

Throughout my journey, I've always enjoyed working with Jeezy. He'll ask certain questions to help pinpoint his message and the best way to get it across. He told me, he needed something different from the norm with a trap/rock feel. This was my fourth time collaborating with the Snowman, and this go-round, I put my stamp on the song titled, "The Realist." We worked more in person and got to play off each other's vibe. I feel like that's important when creating some of your best work. The album debuted at the top spot on the US *Billboard* 200 chart and moved 352,000 copies in the first week. This was Jeezy's first number one album in his career, so this was a special project to be a part of. It always means something to me when I have the opportunity to work multiple times with an artist to create magic. Still, it's even more meaningful when you worked with them at the very start of their professional career because you always have a hand in their success as they grow.

As a producer, you are a scientist, a therapist, and a creative— an architect of sound when it comes to shaping an artist's voice. By this time, the mainstream was catching up to who Jeezy was, and he could've worked with his pick of new production talent, but he wanted to cook up with me again and stay consistent to his sound.

Having, as well as maintaining, excellent relationships are priceless and has always been a key component to my success.

One of my favorite pieces equipment I would love to use was the Roland V-Synth. The original V-Synth was an innovative instrument that combined modeled analogue waveforms and PCM VariPhrase oscillators with user sampling. These audio sources were routed in a semi-modular fashion through a selection of COSM processors such as: standard filters, amp models, waveshapers, side-band filters, frequency shifters, comb filters and more. Features such as the twin D-Beam controllers, 'Time Trip' pad, dedicated knobs and responsive touchscreen ensured that its unique "elastic audio" (as Roland described their 'VariPhrase's concept) was highly malleable in performance. I also used a plug in called Kontakt for the rock guitars and my MPC4000 for the drums and final production of the beat.

Being able to work with the legendary Leslie Braithwaite, Grammy Award winning Audio and Cutting Engineer, producer and composer, born in St. Thomas in the U.S. Virgin Islands, and based in Atlanta— responsible for mixing some of the biggest hits on the charts from the 90s to current including Beyonce, the Migos, Jack Harlow, Pharrell's "Happy," Jeezy's *Thug Motivation 101* album, T.I.'s albums and many more, was definitely a classic moment! The first time we worked was on *Thug Motivation 101*, so it was an amazing opportunity to be included in part 2 of this street novel.

> **The Inspiration** was released on December 12, 2006 by Corporate Thugz Entertainment (CTE) and Def Jam South and debuted on the US Billboard 200 at #1, selling 352,000 copies in that first week. **The Inspiration** was RIAA Gold and Platinum certified on January 23, 2007.

TRACK 10: YOUNG JEEZY

D-BOY TALK

Every time I do something that scares me a little bit, I feel like I don't ever lose even when the outcome may look like failure to the average viewer or thinker.

You can't be successful if you don't take any risks. You've got to think big to receive big. Man.

Don't nobody care about people who always talk about what they're going to do but never pull the trigger. We only respect the shooter or rather the action taker.

Nobody who has accomplished great things did it by playing safe and staying in place. They took a chance, and if they failed or flopped, they progressed in some way.

That "L" was not a loss but a lesson. Your mindset has got to be "go hard or go home."

Photo by Dominic Fondon

TRACK 11

DATE April 10, 2007
ARTIST Boyz N Da Hood
ALBUM *Back Up n da Chevy*
PRODUCED "Paper" featuring Rick Ross

> *"EXCUSES ARE MERELY NAILS USED TO BUILD A HOUSE OF FAILURE."*
> –DRUMMA BOY

The year of 2007 was my "building" year of foundation and I wasn't gonna take steps backward. I could feel the records stacking up like inventory, and I knew I would be ready for anything that came my way. *Back Up n da Chevy* was the second album from Boyz N Da Hood, and I did the track "Paper," featuring Rick Ross. This was a time when Ross just released "Hustlin'" and he was buzzing like crazy. When Big Block had him come by the studio on the Eastside of Atlanta, I wanted to make sure we took advantage of his presence and created something for the streets.

It wasn't the best-selling album of the year, but it was a placement and I always give one hundred and fifty percent no matter what because my name is attached at the end of the day. Of course, I hope that all the projects I'm a part hit gold or platinum status and get millions off streaming, but sometimes it's just as satisfying when the music is heard. There are so many projects that I've produced for or songs I've done that never even came out so it's always exciting when a new project drops and you're on it. I have fun making music, collaborating with these artists, and hope the music touches the people, but more importantly it serves a purpose.

I made this beat on a MPC4000 beat machine and used the Roland rack mount piece for my sounds in the track. Of course, I included the classic "Listen 2 This Track

Bitch" tag, which I would include on my all my street anthems and club bangers. Jody Breeze set the tone and vibe as he was always the go-to for the hooks. Big Ghee started the first verse off followed by Rick Ross. Second verse included another verse from Jody Breeze and Gorilla Zoe. This was one of the songs Big Duke didn't appear on. A lot of times, who ended up on the records really came down to who was in the room that day. If you were in attendance, you had the best chance of being on a song.

I never really realized how many people I helped cope or make it through hard times with this music. People approach me all the time like man, "you helped me thru college" or "I had some of my best times to your music," and that's what keeps you going through the ups and downs. It's always the goal to move and motivate the listening audience and express your true emotions. I want my legacy in my professional and personal life to be about delivering the best quality product, doing above and beyond, being transparent in business, and having integrity in all aspects of life.

> **Back Up n da Chevy** was released on August 7, 2007 through Bad Boy South/Atlantic Records and debuted on the US *Billboard* 200 at #51.

TRACK 11: BOYZ N DA HOOD

D-BOY TALK

It's one thing to be cool when you've got hits, money is flowing in, and everybody is trying to work with you. But what kind of person are you when all that stuff dries up? That's the true test of integrity: who are you without the accolades, praise, and material stuff? Your character is defined when the spotlight is off, and there's nothing to prove.

TRACK 12

DATE May 22, 2007
ARTIST USDA/Young Jeezy
ALBUM *Cold Summer*
PRODUCED "White Girl," "Quickie," and "Go Getta" (remix)

> "BEFORE GPS WE HAD DIRECTIONS. FOLLOW THEM AND YOU MIGHT GET SOMEWHERE."
> —DRUMMA BOY

In the middle of the year in 2007, I'm feeling the momentum and realizing I need more radio singles and songs in the clubs. I always speak on giving one hundred and fifty percent and doing everything possible to reach the next level. When you build up a reputation as someone who delivers results consistently, you will always be in demand. Anytime I had a new batch of music, I would burn a CD, reach out to Jeezy, and link up. I wanted to give him something that was simple but still killed the clubs and airwaves. When I made the "White Girl" beat, I felt like it was something Taylor made for him. Sometimes you don't know how artists gone come on certain beats, but you know they gone rock with it and vibe to it 'til it hit em.

I did three major records on the *Cold Summer* album from USDA, their debut on Jeezy's Corporate Thugz Entertainment label (distributed by Def Jam). The album peaked at #4 on the *Billboard* 200 chart, and "White Girl" was going crazy in the streets and clubs. If it wasn't for Don Imus getting fired from CBS for calling Rutgers women's basketball players "nappy-headed hos" the song might have seen more success. The racial tension hindered the record from reaching its full potential as far as radio airplay and overall support from the label. "Quickie" was a laid-back vibe on the album that the ladies and fellas could vibe to and "Go Getta" remix was a club driven record that featured R. Kelly, Jadakiss, and Bun B.

Going back and putting your guys on that you came up is always something you gotta do in my eyes. Giving the people that helped you an opportunity to live and see their dream come true. Coming from nothing to something you always happy to see more than 10,000 people let alone 100,000 people buy your music. Every 100,000 units you sell generates 1 million dollars and it feels good seeing upcoming artist see their just do from the fans and crowds going crazy at shows. Slick Pulla & Blood Raw gave you different perspective on certain topics and helped complement Jeezy on this album.

Of course, the MPC4000 was the go-to at the time for me and the sounds in this beat I used from the triton. Simple horns and a worm lead instantly gave you an anthem feel followed by the 808 and clap to give it the club bounce. I didn't use a hi-hat because I wanted the track to feel open and give Jeezy the room he needed.

Cold Summer, distributed by Def Jam, debuted at #4 on the US *Billboard* 200. *Cold Summer* made it to #1 on both US *Billboard* Top R&B/Hip Hop Albums and Top Rap Albums. "White Girl", the debut single from the album, peaked at #16 on the US *Billboard* Bubbling Under Hot 100 Singles and peaked at #57 on the US *Billboard* Hot R&B/Hip Hop Songs.

TRACK 12: USDA/YOUNG JEEZY

D-BOY TALK

I've had a few people ask me what I think about all the new producers out here and if I'm threatened by any of them. My response has been the same since I was a youngin' in the game: I'm aware of who is making noise, but I don't compare myself to anybody.

I think if you pay too much attention to who's doing what, you'll start to value your worth by somebody else's standards. I like seeing these guys win—it helps keep the culture alive and thriving, but I focus on what I do. I don't worry about what anybody else is doing.

I read this quote by Matt Gottesman on my Instagram and saved it. I think it fits right here. "Consistency is your way of telling the universe you'll be prepared when your turn is called."

Focus on yourself. So when your time comes, you'll be ready and not getting ready because you were consumed with what everybody else was doing.

Photo by Thomas Jacobi

TRACK 13

DATE August 7, 2007
ARTIST Plies
ALBUM *The Real Testament*
PRODUCED "Shawty" featuring T-Pain

"IF YOU'RE NOT THE TYPE TO LISTEN, NO NEED TO HOLLA AT ME FOR PRODUCTION."
- DRUMMA BOY

I met Plies at S-Line Studios through OG Crip, who was the owner. At the time, it was one of the more popular recording facilities artists used when they came into town to work on new music. Many major labels also leased spaces for their roster of talent who needed to have sessions where a gang of producers would come by and play beats. It was just a special place because everybody fucked with OG Crip, and it was always somebody poppin' in his studio. We exchanged numbers and the first thing I told him was, "I'm gonna change ya life, let's get it."

Six months later, I get a phone call from the rapper, Fiend, at 2 a.m. in the morning like, "come to the studio if you can we need some beats," which happens to be S-Line Studio where we met in the first place. I didn't know if they were for him as an artist or if he was writing for someone, but I know my dawg always a part of something special. What's crazy is I had literally just finished having sex with a young lady like, *damn for real you want me to pull up now?* Lol ... So, I got out the bed, freshened up, and went to the studio cuz you never know what could happen, right? I get to the studio, met up with Fiend and there's an A&R there from Atlantic Records listening to beat packs from producers. He probably went through one hundred beats and an hour went by while we just vibing and the A&R is like damn, "I forgot we got

Drumma Boy in here, play some shit!" You ain't gotta tell me twice. I pushed play immediately! Literally, the fifth beat I played the whole room was like, "yoooooooooo stop what's that?" I played it a few more times and he said, "mark that one." He ended up picking 11 out of 20 beats I played, which ended up landing me a six-song deal with Atlantic Records.

Plies always rapped about "goon this, goon that," so I wanted him to do something different that catered to the ladies, so it was dope to get him on a record with T-Pain, who was also an upcoming Florida bred artist. He was focused, very serious, wasn't telling any jokes, and he certainly wasn't doing too much laughing so it's dope to see him telling jokes daily and entertaining and motivating his fans positively on Instagram and in real life. We can rap about the streets and rap about the hood but we've got to create some music to cater to these women as well. I explained that he needed to make records that would interest these labels and get them excited. And although very rare, he was like, "Shit, I can dig that my nigga, I can dig that."

Then he listened, he took the advice, and ran with it. We had to leak the record cuz the label sent the hook to all the artists on the roster seeing if anyone could come up with a better version. The record started heating up the streets, clubs, and radio stations in Ft. Myers, Orlando, Miami, and surrounding areas in Florida. All of the DJs were going crazy soon as they heard this record and it spread like wildfire. Next thing you know, the label had to support and get behind the record. That's why I look at myself as a conductor. I do more than just make beats; I paint and interpret pictures, in addition to executing plays that will put the artist in a position to win big. The most successful artists are the ones that are coachable. With Plies, the numbers told the story. *The Real Testament* debuted at #2 on the *Billboard* 200 chart with "Shawty" being the lead single and his shows went from $5,000 a show to $50,000 a show.

"Shawty" samples "Fantasy" by Earth, Wind & Fire. Originally Earth, Wind & Fire wanted 100% for the sample but luckily because my mom was cool with Maurice White, they only took 25% once he found out "Billie Gale yo mama," lol.

TRACK 13: PLIES

The Real Testament sold 96,000 units its first week out. It peaked at #2 on the US *Billboard* 200, Top R&B/Hip-Hop Albums and Top Rap Albums. The album was certified gold on February 29, 2008 and certified platinum by the RIAA a little over a decade later on April 8, 2019.

"Shawty" reached #9 on the US *Billboard* Hot 100, #2 on the Hot R&B/Hip-Hop Songs and #1 on both Hot Rap Songs and Rhythmic Charts. As a single, "Shawty" was RIAA certified gold on March 4, 2008 and in 2016 was certified RIAA Platinum. At the time of release, ringtones were all the hype, and by March 2008 the "Shawty" ringtone was certified platinum. "Shawty" won an award for Best Rap/R&B Collaboration at the 2007 Ozone Awards in Houston, TX.

D-BOY TALK

If you don't have a mentor, get one. That's a cheat code. If there isn't anyone you look up to or anyone you can reach out to in your city, read up on somebody who inspires you or listen to interviews of those individuals whose career you admire. But of course, don't get caught up doing exactly what they did because everyone's path is different. Instead, follow the principles because that will develop your character and help you beyond just music or whatever your dream is.

Photo by Azu Visuals

TRACK 14

DATE August 28, 2007
ARTIST Yung Joc
ALBUM *Hustlenomic$*
PRODUCED "Livin' The Life"

"ALWAYS TAKE THE TIME TO PLUG THOSE WHO PLUG YOU."
- DRUMMA BOY

After the success of "Shawty," everybody started reaching out for work. All the labels started flying me into Miami, Los Angeles, and New York for sessions with various artists. In 2006, I met Young Joc at Big Block's studio in Atlanta. Bro was always cool, humble, energetic, and ready to work. Artists that know what they want are usually the most successful.

In 2006, he hit us with "It's Going Down," and that shit seemed to come out of nowhere. I don't think anybody saw that coming. Obviously, the song was an instant and undeniable classic. Still, I think more than anything the success of that record was due just as much to his personality as to the single itself.

He came from a business-minded and hustler's lifestyle. I think that energy penetrated his flow, which made people connect with his movement organically. Joc had the #1 song in the country, and that was just dope to me because I think he understood how to touch the people. He knew how to bring out emotions that made people want to move and dance.

Joc was always a fun person to be around. He always brought this high energy with him, and he was always making people laugh and feel good. And he put that in his music. It was always an experience working with him, and it's a good feeling for me that I was a part of his career journey as an artist. When we recorded "Livin' The Life," I started making a beat, and one of my writer homies, Ebony Love, was mumbling melodies. I couldn't make out the words, but I loved the pattern she was doing. I nodded my head at her like that's it and she slowly filled in the words, which is the hook we hear today!

What's also crazy to me about Joc is that Gorilla Zoe learned a lot from being around him; many artists did. Joc was like a teacher; he was inspiring all the other artists at that time, and I remember him telling Zoe like, "Dawg, all you got to do is keep doing this, keep doing this." When Zoe listened to the things Joc suggested, he put out a record out called "Hood Nigga" in 2007, and that song became one of Zoe's major hits.

So, in my opinion, Joc was always trying to help people get on and teach them how to do things the right way. He was like a big brother to Block's label.

Yung Joc's *Hustlenomics*, released by Bad Boy Records, sold 70,000 copies that first week and debuted at #3 on the *Billboard* 200. It peaked at #1 on both the Top R&B/Hip-Hop Albums and Top Rap Albums.

TRACK 14: YUNG JOC

D-BOY TALK

There aren't any more gatekeepers in music. Let that marinate in your spirit and motivate your mind to create some dope art. The people, as in your fan base, are the new A&R's. The culture dictates who and what's hot. Also, let this information eliminate making excuses. Stop worrying about the wrong things, the stuff that has nothing to do with what you're trying to accomplish. Just create good shit, and everything else will come as a result of that.

TRACK 15

DATE Sept 25, 2007
ARTIST Gorilla Zoe
ALBUM Welcome to the Zoo
PRODUCED "Do Something," "Crack Muzik" featuring Jody Breeze, "Juice Box" featuring Yung Joc, and "Lil Shawty"

> "I'D RATHER WORK WITH A TALENTED ARTIST WITH NO SOCIAL MEDIA BUZZ WHO LISTENS."
> -DRUMMA BOY

I remember riding in the car with Gorilla Zoe, and this was before he even signed to Block. He asked my opinion about whether I think he should sign over there. My response went something like this, "Man, somebody is giving you an opportunity. Why would you not do it, especially if it's your ONLY opportunity?"

Block was replacing Jeezy with Zoe after Jeezy embarked on his solo career. Many people didn't understand it at first. They were like, "This is who you're getting to replace Jeezy?"

But Zoe had been through similar shit; he'd experienced and seen a lot of those same situations. I don't think people knew this because Zoe didn't roll with a crew and wasn't as vocal about that kind of stuff. From a street's perspective, the only thing Zoe didn't have was the money, the street fame, or recognition that Jeezy had as a trap artist.

All those questions and speculations got put to bed when he came out with "Hood Nigga." It was his 'shut everybody up' record. He then returned with "Lost," and everybody thought the record was too slow and that it wasn't going to work. Lil Wayne jumped on it, and the song landed at #10 on the *Billboard* chart.

Everybody was like, "How did they get Wayne on that song?"

Of course, everybody was fucking with it after that but didn't understand the song before then. That's why you've got to believe in what feels right in your gut and not switch up. You've got to, figuratively speaking, be ready to live and die by your decisions. Whether it hit or fall short of your expectations, you've got to stand by the outcome. Everybody's not going to co-sign you until someone they revere co-sign you. Those people are not part of your core tribe. As soon as another artist comes along with a hot song, they will jump on that bandwagon.

So, stay tapped into your Day Ones; they'll be your evangelists, telling other people about your music and turning them into fans. I saw all the success that Zoe and I had together, and I also saw him out on the road with Flo Rida doing amazing things.

When the opportunity presents itself, you've got to get your ass in however you can get your ass in. If an honorable person approaches you, someone who will give you a situation and put some money behind it, you can't turn that down. Gorilla Zoe had gone from being just another dope ass rapper from the street to a millionaire. So, it's just good to see guys follow their dreams and get to it. When everybody hate you or when everybody doubt you, you need to see the bigger picture.

As long as you can visualize what can be and become blind to what is, that's when people like myself recognize this faith and will come in to help not only the talented but deserving artists expand their vision.

Welcome to the Zoo, released on September 25, 2007, debuted at #18 on the US *Billboard* 200 charts. The album reached #8 on the Top R&B/Hip-Hop Albums and #3 Top Rap Albums. *Welcome to the Zoo* featured two singles, "Hood Nigga" and "Juice Box" featuring Yung Joc.

TRACK 15: GORILLA ZOE

D-BOY TALK

DON'T WANT THE LIFESTYLE AND FAME SO BAD THAT YOU BURN BRIDGES TO GET IT BECAUSE THERE'S NO DOUBLING BACK ONCE THAT MATCH IS LIT. KEEP YOUR INTEGRITY AT ALL COSTS AND ON EVERY LEVEL. ALSO, NEVER GET COMFORTABLE— STAY HUNGRY, AND PAY WHATEVER DUES YOU'VE GOTTA PAY. YOU WILL ALWAYS GET BACK WHAT YOU PUT IN, AND USUALLY YOU'LL REAP WAY MORE THAN WHAT YOU SOW.

TRACK 16

DATE October 30, 2007
ARTIST Playaz Circle
ALBUM *Supply & Demand*
PRODUCED "We Workin"

"IF THEY TRY TO SLOW YOU DOWN, SPEED UP. THE OBJECTIVE IS TO WIN."
—DRUMMA BOY

When I worked with Playaz Circle, you could tell 2 Chainz was already a star. He was going under the name Tity Boi at the time. We talked a lot, mostly about music business stuff, but also life. We were like brothers, and his people would always come over to my crib to work. I'm sure everybody peep it now, but he's always been a really intelligent dude, very intentional and strategic in whatever he did.

I always had an open-door studio policy with Tity Boi or whomever he was rolling with, so whenever they wanted to come over to the house to record, they were always welcomed. He'd bring in other producers and work on projects because he was always frustrated with the label's politics. He didn't feel like he was being supported enough, but the good thing was he had the money to invest in himself, which he did.

He had the song "Duffle Bag Boy" out with Lil Wayne, but many people thought it was Wayne's record. This was 2007, and Wayne was on fire, so people identified him before they did Tity Boi. During one of our talks, I advised him to consider reinventing himself and come up with a new name or a different alias. When we did that *T.R.U. Religion* project in 2011, he said he was about to go ahead and call himself 2 Chainz.

I was like, "2 Chainz?! That shit is hard right there."

And it's crazy because a lot of these genius ass conversations were had in the studio and just being goofy as hell, was when he confirmed his name. I knew that would be it for him, and we ended up doing the record "Boo," which helped to introduce his new name and the rebirth of his career.

When he rapped, "I just call her boo, I don't know her whole name keep it on the low, mayne, all I eat it is lo mein," I remembered saying, "Woooo bruh, this shit reminds me of some college shit. College students are going to love this record because all they eat is lo mein. Dudes from the trap are going to love this record. When you're broke, and you're trying to keep that budget down, you're about to get you some lo mein, add some water, and be cool."

I told him he had to put Yo Gotti on the record. I always tell artists that Memphis is a tri-state region. That's where everybody comes to break their record outside of Atlanta in the south. You've got three states, and we call it the ATM trifecta: Arkansas, Tennessee, and Mississippi. So, when people spin your records in Memphis, you're getting a look in the tri-state regions with millions and millions of people. Memphis went crazy for that record, and 2 Chainz stayed booked.

To me, that's where his career took off. Then Atlanta started playing it, and every other major urban market jumped on board by spinning it as well. We followed it up with the track "Spend It." That one simple line, "I'm riding round, and I'm getting it," became a hit within itself because a lot of people related to that sentiment. With "Boo" peaking at #76 on the Hot R&B/Hip-Hop charts and then "Spend It" making it to the #55 position on the same chart, I saw this as a definite blessing to deliver on the records that helped put him on.

Those two records helped set him up for his first official single, "No Lie," in 2012 with Drake. Once you get that song with Drake, you're out of here.

Supply & Demand, released on Disturbing tha Peace (DTP) and Def Jam South and debuted at #27 on the US *Billboard* 200. The album also reached #3 on Top R&B/Hip-Hop Albums and #1 US Top Rap Albums charts.

TRACK 16: PLAYAZ CIRCLE

D-BOY TALK

Every day you've got decisions to make. Make beats or make excuses. Workout or start 'tomorrow.' Get up early or sleep in. Go out or stay in to handle business. Stack money or spend it. Read a book or watch TV. Eat clean or eat the wings and fries.

These seemingly insignificant everyday decisions add up to weeks, months, and years that create your life. Weigh every decision by asking yourself if what you're deciding is moving you closer to or further away from your goals. It doesn't seem like a big deal at the moment, but trust me, it all counts.

Decide your day in advance by planning out how you're going to spend your resources. If you challenge yourself to do this for one month, I promise the difference it makes will alter your life.

Until you change, nothing will change.

TRACK 17

DATE December 4, 2007
ARTIST DJ Drama
ALBUM Gangsta Grillz The Album
PRODUCED "Gangsta Grillz" featuring Lil Jon and "187" featuring Project Pat, B.G., 8Ball & MJG

> "STAYING READY IS WHAT KEEPS OPPORTUNITIES COMING IN STEADY."
> -DRUMMA BOY

When I first moved to Atlanta, I did some production work with an emerging record label called Black Out Music. They had more of a low key than a movement BMF in terms of being flashy, but they were well represented in the city and made real plays like bosses. They invested in their artists like a major as well. Their whole roster of talent was tight: Rob Jackson, Charlie Hustle, and Fiona Simone.

When they brought me on-board, the first order of business was to give them heat for a Gangsta Grillz's mixtape they wanted to put out to introduce their camp. The CEO knew I'd just relocated from Memphis and hadn't established a permanent residence, so he had his staff put me up in a mansion for six months. They treated a brother like a king. They also wanted me to focus and go in on the project since they had a lot of money riding on it.

This was the first Gangsta Grillz's mixtape I did in my life. Unfortunately, none of the artists on the tape blew up like I thought or had hoped. But the beats I did on that project attracted a lot of attention in the industry, namely DJ Drama, who was quietly scouting production talent for his project.

After doing "Standing Ovation" for Jeezy and "Shawty" for Plies, I was hell-bent on getting another hit song. That's why I was so hungry to get in with Drama because not only did I respect his contributions to the culture, but he also had all the plugs. Relationships are everything to me inside as well as outside of the business. They are the name of the game. Every placement and every album I've ever been on is because I knew the artist— simple.

I came up in the industry with Gotti. When I call, he's going to pick up the phone. When I call Jeezy, he's going to pick up the phone. Keep in mind that I didn't come up in the world of A&R's, management, and emailing beats. That's not where I came from; that's not my story. Back then, all transactions were being handled in cash. I used to pull up on Gotti at the gas station in Memphis— the Chevron to be exact. He'd buy ten beats at a time and cash me out.

When I think back on it now, I'm sure some folks thought we were doing drug deals. It's an entirely different world now, and this is the digital generation. I'm thankful for the advancements, but you can never replace human interaction with technology. You've got to be willing to get out there and meet people and shake hands. That's how I was able to lock in and build with Drama.

I stayed busy when I touched down in ATL because there were many people to work with, unlike in Memphis. Don't get me wrong, my city-bred some legendary talent, but you could count on your hand how many artists we had. There was Jeezy, T.I.P., 2 Chainz, Migos, Outkast, and Goodie Mob as well as the artists that came out of those camps like Sleepy Brown, Cee-Lo, and Andre 3000. Everywhere I went, there was just so many damn people to get bread with. People were reaching out by hitting my line, or I'd have run-ins at the studio or the club.

'Let me get something from you, Drumma. I need to get that ASAP and money ain't no issue.'

You'd thought I was selling crack the way people were feigning for my beats. From major label artists coming into town like Drake, Plies, Birdman, and Rick Ross, before buying a crib here, to people already in the city like Block ENT and DJ Drama; I was securing the bag before that phrase became a thing. I'm going to always go to where the work is and set up shop where there is a bag consistently coming in. That's how I got the nickname D-Boy Fresh.

TRACK 17: DJ DRAMA

People would always say I stayed fresh because I knew how to work the system to my advantage and get paid, which kept my wardrobe on point.

Atlanta is also one of those cities where everybody wants to associate with you once you get into the matrix. Still, my involvement comes with a price attached to it. I grew up listening to the Gangsta Grillz's brand. I was a fan of the movement, so to have a solid relationship with Drama is a blessing that I don't take lightly.

> *Gangsta Grillz: The Album*, released on December 4, 2007, was the debut album from DJ Drama and was executive produced by T.I.. It reached #26 on the US *Billboard* 200, #2 on the Top Rap Albums, #3 on Top R&B/Hip-Albums, #29 on the Comprehensive Albums and #7 on the Top Tastemaker Albums charts.

D-BOY TALK

I DEFINE ENTREPRENEURSHIP AS BEING ABLE TO DO WHAT I WANT TO DO WHEN I WANT TO DO IT. I THINK THE WAY YOU LIVE DURING YOUR LIFETIME IS IF YOU TAKE ALL OF THE GREAT IDEAS YOU HAVE AND EXECUTE THEM BECAUSE WE'RE ONLY YOUNG ONCE AND ONLY HERE ONCE (THAT WE KNOW OF).

AS WE ALL MATURE AND GET OLDER, YOU WANT TO MAKE SURE YOU ARE TAKING ADVANTAGE OF THE TIME YOU'VE BEEN GIVEN.

I'VE SEEN HOW SHORT LIFE IS FOR A LOT OF PEOPLE. I MEAN, IN THE TIME IT TAKES TO SNAP YOUR FINGERS, THINGS CAN GO WRONG. I'VE KNOWN PEOPLE WHO HAVE SUFFERED FROM TERRIBLE ACCIDENTS AND GO FROM BEING AT THE PEAK OF THEIR LIFE TO LYING IN A HOSPITAL BED.

EVERY DAY, WHILE I'M HERE, I'M WORKING.

BUT WHAT ACTUALLY MAKES ME HAPPY ABOUT MAKING MONEY IS WITNESSING PEOPLE HAPPY TO SPEND IT WITH ME. THAT'S WHY I DO THIS, FOR PEOPLE TO JOYFULLY BREAK BREAD WITH ME BECAUSE THEY KNOW THEY ARE MAKING A WISE INVESTMENT AND TRUST ME TO DELIVER THEM THE BEST THAT I'VE GOT. THEY KNOW HOW HARD I GO, SO THAT GIVES THEM THE CONFIDENCE TO TRUST IN ME.

THERE WAS A TIME WHEN I WAS UNDERPAID; MANY OF US AS PRODUCERS AND CREATIVES HAVE DONE A LOT OF SHIT THAT DIDN'T REFLECT OUR REAL VALUE.

WE'VE GIVEN THESE ARTISTS SWAG, A VIBE, ENERGY, THE JUICE, A LOOK, AND HOOKS. I CHALKED IT ALL UP TO PAYING MY DUES, BUT ONCE I GREW MY RESUME TO THAT 'FUCK YOU PAY ME' STATUS, THAT'S THE MENTALITY I'VE BEEN ON UNLESS I DECIDE OTHERWISE.

THAT'S THE BEAUTY OF BEING AN ENTREPRENEUR.

YOU GET TO CHOOSE.

Photo by Dominic Fondon

TRACK 18

DATE December 4, 2007
ARTIST Scarface
ALBUM *Made*
PRODUCED "Never"

> "PEOPLE WILL SAY ANYTHING TO MAKE THEMSELVES LOOK GOOD. THE EGO IS A HELLUVA DRUG."
> - DRUMMA BOY

After working with Tela and the Rap-A-Lot label in 2002, Slim Thug in 2004 and Paul Wall in 2007, I had a growing fan base out in Texas. My brother also had a strong relationship with Scarface and always told him that he should work with me. I got a call from Redboy one day saying that he needed some beats for an upcoming album that Scarface was working on. Once he sent his email, I may have sent around 5 to 10 tracks. About two weeks later he called back letting me know Scarface recorded to one of the beats and that he wanted to use the song for the album. All I could think was, "wow imma be on a Scarface album and I'm not even 25 yet!"

This particular beat I made on the MPC4000 and I sampled "Sara Smile" by Ronnie Dyson. I wanted to create something that would show off my crate digging skills and please the true hip hop heads from around the world, especially in New York. When I first heard the song and how Face was speaking on never violating the code, I knew this would be a classic in the streets. The key for producers is to always hear the best rappers in the game over your beats. You have to picture it in your head and for some reason that has helped me carve out some of the biggest beats I've ever produced.

Made, Scarface's ninth studio album, was released by Rap-A-Lot Records, Asylum Records, and Atlantic Records on December 4, 2007. The album reached #17 on the US *Billboard* 200 and #2 on the Top R&B/Hip-Hop Albums.

D-BOY TALK

SOMETIMES NOBODY'S AROUND TO HEAR YOU OUT. BUT THAT MICROPHONE GONE LISTEN TO YOU.

Photo by Dominic Fondon

TRACK 19

DATE March 11, 2008
ARTIST Rick Ross/Rozay
ALBUM *Trilla*
PRODUCED "Money Make Me Come" featuring Ebony Love and "Here I Am" featuring Nelly, Avery Storm

> "PEOPLE WILL SAY ANYTHING TO MAKE THEMSELVES LOOK GOOD. THE EGO IS A HELLUVA DRUG."
> —DRUMMA BOY

I met E-Class, the founder of Po Boy Music Group, on a trip to Florida that Atlantic Records had set up for me. I was in town to work with Flo Rida, but the label ended up asking me to stay. That way, I could collaborate with the other talents they had on the roster who were also working on projects. I'm never the one that will say no because you don't know where your blessings and the next big opportunities will come from. And being that this business is so fickle, you've really got to take advantage of situations when they present themselves.

They ended up putting me in the studio with Rick Ross. He had just dropped "Hustling," which was a huge hit, but that was the only song he had out. I trusted E-Class, and I was meeting with him out of that respect, but I also knew from that one single that Ross had the potential to be huge. I don't look at rappers as being one-hit-wonders. I don't even think like that because if you're a new artist and you're doing your thing, and I work with you, I'm going to either make you hot or keep you there.

I think that's the level of creative genius I have because it makes me no difference whether you're a well-known artist or not. I don't give a fuck about that shit. That's always been my attitude and approach. Just cut the check and watch me make your artist blow up. Look at what I did for Drake. Who the fuck knew him before me, before "Money To Blow?" I'm not speaking on his visibility as an actor on Degrassi. I mean, coming out as a rapper with a real viable record that resonated with the culture. He didn't have any music out. He wasn't even Drake at the time; he was just the kid from that television series. Having a name never matters to me; if I'm on the team, I will change your life.

Ross was a cool cat, fly as hell, and he just had a vision. Again, it's the mindset. It's certain people who have the mindset and understand what it takes to not just get a hit but also know how to repeat that winning system; that's the secret and the answer. Certain individuals know what the fuck they want and have got their shit together, so by them being so confident, you just know they are going to be somebody.

We did a few records but it was when Ross came to Atlanta where he ended up recording two hard records for his album *Trilla* that showcased his clever wordplay and rap delivery as well as his business savvy. I got a call from Julia Beverly that Ross was in town and they were at Patchwerk Studio working. When I got there, Ross told me to plug in and play something special. I wanted him to see what I had done with my band Drumma Boy Live so I played those tracks first and he was like, "yoooooo I got somebody for this." He called Avery Storm and sent him the beat I just played. A few hours later, Avery sent a hook back, which was "Here I Am," and the rest was history. Ross went in the booth and the first words you here are "Ricky Ross... this something special right here." By the time he finished his verse, I knew this would be a ladies' anthem. Nelly's feature solidified that. The second record I did on the album was "Money Make Me Come," which Ebony love did the hook and my boy Tomcat engineered the session. Tomcat happens to be Rozay's full-time engineer now!

From his debut album to this one, you can hear his growth and maturity. Again, his mindset is so powerful. You can tell that he had this mental shift; he had read more, he studied more, he knew how to navigate the politics of the industry, and he kept people around him that would push him in the right direction. Not everybody does that or has that support system. That takes a strong mentality, which defines who you are as a person— who you are with the decisions that you make. His success as a thought leader is much bigger than his success as just Ross the rapper. He's like a preacher in a pulpit, except his congregation is the streets.

TRACK 19: RICK ROSS

Trilla is Rick Ross's second studio album, released by Slip-n-Slide Records, Def Jam South Recordings and Poe Boy Entertainment on March 11, 2008. In its first week *Trilla* sold 198,000 copies landing it at #1 on the US *Billboard* 200. In its second week it sold 90,000 copies and by May 8, 2008 was certified gold by the RIAA. *Trilla* also hit #1 on the Top R&B/Hip-Hop Albums and Top Rap Albums charts.

"Here I Am", the third single from *Trilla*, made it to #41 on the US *Billboard* Hot 100, #5 on Hot Rap Songs chart, #9 on the Hot R&B/Hip-Hop Songs as well as #12 on the US Rhythmic chart, "Here I Am" also made an appearance on the Pop 100, peaking at #86.

D-BOY TALK

DON'T FOLLOW THE TRENDS, BUT INSTEAD SET THEM. THAT'S HOW YOU MAKE A NAME FOR YOURSELF AND STAND OUT. ONCE EVERYBODY STARTS DOING SOMETHING OR USING A CERTAIN SOUND, THE COOL FACTOR IS OVER.

TRACK 20

DATE March 18, 2008
ARTIST Rocko
ALBUM *Self-Made*
PRODUCED "Umma Do Me," "Tomorrow," "Busy," "Old Skool," "Like This Here," "Snakes," "Meal," "Thugs Need Love Too" featuring Monica

> *"ALWAYS SEEK RESPECT, NOT ATTENTION."*
> – DRUMMA BOY

At this particular juncture in my career, I had worked with legends I'd grown up listening to like Scarface "Never" and 8Ball & MJG "Give me that Grey Goose" and "Put That Yak Back" as well as rising stars Jeezy "Standing Ovation," and Jody Breeze "Get Ya Gangsta On." I decided to get some flyers made and commissioned a local Black-owned business, Mark Star Graphics, located right next door to where Big Boi's Purple Ribbon label used to be in Atlanta.

I had the whole Drum Squad Productions family take a group photo outside of Mark's building in black t-shirts with the slogan *Got Beats?* on the front that I jacked from the *Got Milk?* ad. I put that image on the front of the flyer, and I listed my entire resume along with a discography of the songs I'd made for people on the back. I also had my name and number listed on them and passed those flyers out all over the city. This was during an era when club promoters would be in the streets heavy, passing out flyers for the hottest nightspots. I saw it as a way to put my name and likeness in everybody's face and hands just like they were doing.

My hustle have always been on another level. I've always been hungry, and even to this day, I'm always thinking of ways to brand and separate myself from other creatives in the game. That's been another secret to my success. You've got to stay diversifying yourself, and despite how big you get, you've got to continue to let people know who you are and what you've done as well as what you're doing.

You can never assume that everybody knows you because they don't. There are new teenagers every day who are just learning about the generation of artists and producers before them. You've got to also remember that there are more people outside of your backyard, city, state, and country.

Sometimes when we're popping in one place, we can fall under the spell of our ego and forget it's a big planet filled with folks who have yet to discover you. Get into having an international mindset. You never know where your fans and supporters will come from; embrace them all.

So, I had these flyers circulating everywhere, and I had printed the lyrics from some of the more popular songs that people were familiar with like "White Girl." Before it became mainstream, I had my actual phone number printed on them, too, and it would just be blowing up.

And then one day out of the blue, I got a message from Rocko. I remember him saying, "Man, I just got your flyer from this barbershop. I see the songs you produced, man; you work hard. I like the work you're doing, and I want to get some shit from ya."

I loved the challenge, so I couldn't wait to catch up with this dude. We're going back and forth phone tagging and whatnot for a minute until we finally caught up with each other. I loved having that energy again and that he knew what he wanted to accomplish with his music. It was just a fantastic opportunity to catch an artist like him at that beginning phase of his career and be able to come through.

It was crazy in the streets, too, at the time. I believe he had just lost one of his main men— one of his homies, and he was serious about going all-in with music and make something happen. And to be able to deliver something at such a high level to somebody during a critical moment in time is priceless.

Rocko wanted to set up a session, and the first place we worked was 11th Street Studios, which is located off 11th Street in Atlanta's West Midtown area. I think at that time, Josh Butler owned the studio; he was super cool and ran the place like a corporate company with a professional environment.

TRACK 20: ROCKO

The day we went in, I didn't have any preconceived ideas about a sound other than I wanted the beat to have a certain rawness to it as well as an attitude. I wanted to create something fresh, based on our vibe and chemistry. I had to deliver, but I knew that I would because I told him that I'd change his life if he worked with me. I tell everybody I work with that because that's genuinely how I feel with the right combination.

The first song we recorded was "Umma Do Me." I remember when he rapped the words, *"You just do you, umma do me,"* from the booth that we had something. To the average ear, the words might've sounded simple, but I felt his soul on so many levels because it was more about the delivery.

As an artist, you've got to believe the words for them to connect with your audience, and that's what he did. Rocko was a natural on the mic, very charismatic. He was confident in how he rhymed because he was spitting shit that was true to him, his reality, or in today's popularized terminology— he was "speaking his truth." He had an independent, entrepreneurial, and rebel spirit, which came through when combined with my beats. He rhymed like he had something to prove; he did, and so did I. Most people outside of Atlanta only know about Rocko as a rapper, but back then, people associated his name with being a street dude who had recently started a label.

I used to ask people, "Y'all heard of an artist named Rocko?"

The general response was usually, "Yeah, we know Rocko, but he's an executive with a label and is signing artists. What's he doing rapping?"

Nobody could believe that he was actually in the booth recording. I took that as a personal challenge and wanted to be the one who could prove that I had the power to take an exec, give him a sound, and have the whole world bopping to our music. All the things that were challenging in my career gave me my biggest results. I liked working with Rocko; he was just so cool, and his flow matched his personality.

I've never wanted to take the easy route right out of the gate and work with the Jay-Z's and Beyoncé's of the world because whatever record they put out, it's going to blow. So, aligning my talents with a guy like Rocko gave me a strategic platform for me to be able to continue working with all these artists that people have never heard of and make them stars.

There's no glory in giving the superstar a hit record, but your whole career can shift if you do that for an underdog. So, Rocko and I did "Umma Do Me," and I got a kick out of the process. He was enthusiastic and fun to record with. He reminded me a lot of Gucci Mane from the perspective of his mindset and knowing what he wanted. Rocko is a stand-up guy. When he says he's going to do something, he's going to do it. And that goes so far, especially with relationships in this music industry.

> *Self-Made,* Rocko's first studio album debuted at #21 on the US *Billboard* 200. *Self-Made* reached #6 on the US Top R&B/Hip-Hop Albums and #4 on the Top Rap Albums charts.

TRACK 20: ROCKO

D-BOY TALK

THE BEST THING ABOUT EARNING SUCCESS IS THAT IF YOU HANDLE YOUR OPPORTUNITIES CORRECTLY, THEY KEEP ON COMING. THAT'S WHY YOU'LL NOTICE HOW I REPEATEDLY SAY RELATIONSHIPS ARE KEY. AND IT'S ABOUT THE QUALITY OVER THE QUANTITY. I HAVE FORMED BONDS WITH HOLLYWOOD ACTORS, THEIR AGENTS, INDIVIDUALS THAT OWN LIQUOR COMPANIES, CLOTHING DESIGNERS, PAINTERS, ART GALLERY OWNERS, ETC. WHEN I HAVE AN IDEA THAT I'M READY TO EXECUTE, I HAVE A PLETHORA OF PEOPLE I CAN CALL ON AND GREEN LIGHT MY VISION. THERE'S A DIRECT LINE OF COMMUNICATION WITH THE MAN OR WOMAN WHO CAN MAKE IT HAPPEN.

Photo by Tony Tyus

TRACK 21

DATE Sept. 2, 2008
ARTIST Young Jeezy
ALBUM *The Recession*
PRODUCED "Put On" featuring Kanye West, "Hustlaz Ambition" and "Amazin"

> *"IF YOU'RE NOT OK OR COMFORTABLE WITH BEING MISUNDERSTOOD, DON'T GET INTO THE ENTERTAINMENT BUSINESS."*
> — DRUMMA BOY

From the get-go, Jeezy told me that if I came through for him on "Standing Ovation" for *Thug Motivation 101*, we would be locked in forever. He had experienced crazy success with his mixtapes. Still, there was a lot of expectation riding on his mainstream debut to exceed or at the very least match the energy he had with his music that had been circulating in the streets. So, when I delivered that heat, we had a tight bond from that day forward, and he stayed true to his word about locking in.

So, he hit me up about beats for *The Recession*, and we went on to do the single "Put On" with Kanye. I remember being pissed off during the making of this record because I did the beat at the house. I was thinking I had to come up with a bigger song than the old school Chicago anthem when the Bulls would come out on the court. That was on my mind heavy; that need to craft something that would be a new anthem for the city of Chicago and the cities of the fans that would be consuming the music. That became my inspiration and vision throughout the entire creative process. It's all I thought about. You could even say I was lightweight obsessed. Still, I knew that if I could pull this off as I envisioned it, it'd be a huge victory for me, and everybody involved.

Once I felt satisfied with the beat, I sent the record in but didn't hear anything back as fast as I wanted. Naturally, that made me anxious. Jeezy ended up texting me, saying that he had something crazy for me, but before we spoke, Mz. Shyneka, a local personality on the radio station Hot 107.9, premiered the record.

When I heard it, all I could say was, "Oh my God."

It was crazy, man. Kanye came in with the auto-tune, and I was like, "This shit is crazy! Kanye is rapping on my beat!"

It was just the energy he brought, and then to have Jay-Z jump on the remix was phenomenal. Everywhere I go, that's one of the biggest songs I get credit for to date. So, it's just a great blessing to be a part of a musical legacy that masses of people who genuinely love these records remember. By the way, I also constructed the beats for "Hustlaz Ambition" and "Amazin'" from *The Recession*, which sat at #1 on the *Billboard* 200 chart when it debuted and has since become certified gold.

> **"Put On"** was released on June 3, 2008, as *The Recession*'s lead single. It received a Grammy nomination for Best Rap Performance by a Duo or Group, peaked at #12 on the US *Billboard* Hot 100 and was certified platinum by April 2010. The ringtone was certified platinum in December 2009. The song eventually certified 3x platinum by the RIAA in June 2020.

In an interview with Billboard, I explained the creation of the beat. "I think about the process of making the beat. I remember being at my crib and I was arguing with somebody and pissed off about something. Jeezy just reached out about needing some beats, "I need them yams." I was in the perfect mood. I remember being home alone and it was probably around 3 a.m. and I started making the beat. I turned off all the lights and got the feeling I did when I was a kid walking into the studio for the first time and seeing all the different lights, meters flashing, computer on desktop mode and everything was just a vibe. I rolled up a couple blunts and lit up the first one to get in the zone. The first sounds I played made me feel like I was in The Twilight Zone. When I first made the "Put On" beat, I wanted it to feel like a new anthem for the Chicago Bulls when they came out on the floor. I was thinking about the Bulls anthem with Phil Jackson and Michael Jordan in primetime. I made that beat in 30 minutes and put it into Pro Tools and sent it over to Jeezy fresh off the press.

TRACK 21: YOUNG JEEZY

"Put On" took on a life of its own with an official remix featuring Jay-Z, released on July 29, 2008. The beat sparked creativity among other artists as well, with Ludacris, Lil Wayne, Trae tha Truth, Rick Ross, Ace Hood, Plies, Wale, and The-Dream all dropping their own freestyles over it.

> *The Recession* was released on September 2, 2008 and debuted at #1 on the US *Billboard* 200 and was certified RIAA Gold on December 10, 2008. By October 2009, *The Recession* had sold 886,000 copies. On July 2, 2020 the album became officially certified RIAA Platinum.

D-BOY TALK

I'M A KNOWN STUDIO RAT. THAT'S WHERE I SPENT THE MAJORITY OF MY LATE TEENS AND TWENTIES. BUT I'M GOING TO SAY THIS: DON'T FORGET TO LIVE LIFE. TO STAY CREATIVE. WE'VE GOT TO SEE NEW THINGS, HEAR NEW SOUNDS, MEET NEW PEOPLE, AND HAVE NEW CONVERSATIONS.

I TAKE VACATIONS NOW, SOMETHING I USED TO NOT DO. I EXPERIENCE EVERYTHING THE ENVIRONMENT AND CULTURE OFFERS. I LISTEN TO OTHER MUSIC OUTSIDE OF HIP-HOP AND RAP JUST TO HEAR HOW OTHER GENRES STRUCTURE SONGS.

YOU'VE GOT TO WORK, YES, BUT YOU'VE ALSO GOT TO HAVE NEW EXPERIENCES TO KEEP YOUR ARTISTIC JUICES FLOWING.

Photo by Justin Trout

TRACK 22

DATE September 30, 2008
ARTIST T.I.
ALBUM Paper Trail
PRODUCED "What Up, What's Haapnin'," "Ready For Whatever," "My Life Your Entertainment" featuring Usher, "You Ain't Missin Nothing"

"GREAT WORK USUALLY GOES TO THE INDIVIDUALS WHO PROVE THEIR ABILITY TO HANDLE ORDINARY WORK WITH EXCELLENCE AND WITHOUT COMPLAINT."
— DRUMMA BOY

Being prepared when an opportunity presents itself is the key to having success. When I moved to Atlanta from Memphis, one of the first people I met was Jason Geter, the business partner, and manager of T.I.P. Of course, I wanted to work with the westside rapper, but the timing never seemed right for us to connect. So, I would go to each and every album release that T.I would do so I could really studio his sound, the type of beats he selected, and to get as familiar as possible with his music so I would be able to catch the next album.

One of the things I learned early on in this business was the ability to have an unusual amount of patience. Every collab I've done that felt forced when the artist was overreaching to link or vice versa; nothing ever seemed to go right. The chemistry between you and the talent must have a natural flow; it needs to be a proper fit. You've got to be persistent and aggressive, but not to the point where you become annoying. That balancing act is a skill; master it. One of the things I've noticed over the years is that the more alike the artist and producer's work ethic is, the better the fit, for obvious reasons. Never work with people who don't value your time, which is one of the highest forms of disrespect.

Remember when I said that Rocko reached out because he saw one of my flyers with the songs I'd done listed on it? Well, check this out. During this time, T.I.P. was in prison but had been watching Rocko's whole process going from an executive businessman to behind the mic and how I was the one who helped blow him up. It just goes to show that when you bless somebody else's life, that blessing comes back tenfold.

So, I get a call not long after T.I.P. came home about doing some work on his sixth album, *Paper Trail*. I remember it was crazy because I had to sign up and go through this approval process to visit T.I.P. at his house. I was one of his first visitors. As soon as I walked up, he was at the door to greet me.

"What's up, King," I say.

He responds by saying something to the effect of, "Naw man, you the king! You blessed my boy. Everything you did for Rocko I need that!"

It blew my mind at how the hype of what I did for Rocko was still significantly impacting my career. That's why it's essential to approach anything you attach your name to with the highest level of excellence and pride. Somebody out there is paying attention.

T.I.P. went on to say, "I've got to have you on my album."

I could sense he wanted to get cooking "ASAP" to release the creative energy he had built up while serving his time. I played around thirty beats during our meeting. He picked out twenty-seven, and I ended up having four songs on the album. It was such a blessing to be able to deliver again at such a high level with an iconic artist I'd wanted to get in with for years. Paper Trail, to date, is T.I.P.'s most successful album.

I also produced "My Life Your Entertainment" featuring Usher and "You Ain't Missing Nothing," which Whitney Houston also used for song called "Salute" shortly after on her album *I Look To You*.

TRACK 22: T.I.

"What Up, What's Haapnin'," released on September 2, 2008 was the fifth single from T.I.'s album, *Paper Trail*. The record slid into the US *Billboard* Hot 100 at #84 and topped off the Hot Raps Songs chart at #34. The official video was released a couple weeks later on iTunes and made its way to BET's 106 & Park and MTV.

"Ready for Whatever" was the sixth single released from *Paper Trail*. on September 23, 2008. "Ready For Whatever" peaked at #57 on the US *Billboard* Hot 100 and #62 on the Canadian Hot 100.

Paper Trail, T.I.'s sixth studio album, was released on September 30, 2008 and sold 568,000 copies in the first week. This album had the fourth highest debut of 2008 and became T.I.'s third consecutive US #1 debut. The album spent 55 weeks on the US *Billboard* charts and was certified Platinum December 15, 2008. On August 26, 2009, *Paper Trail* was certified RIAA 2x Platinum.

D-BOY TALK

THE BIGGER YOUR THINKING GETS, THE BIGGER THE SIZE OF YOUR ACCOMPLISHMENTS. GET A RIDICULOUSLY AMBITIOUS VISION FOR YOUR LIFE AND ONLY SPEAK AND WRITE WORDS THAT REFLECT THE SUCCESS YOU WANT. DON'T EVER SELL YOURSELF SHORT. YOU'VE GOT TO TRUST YOURSELF ON THE DARKEST OF NIGHTS AND KEEP PUSHING THROUGH. WHEN YOU ACT CONFIDENTLY, YOUR THOUGHTS GO IN THE SAME DIRECTION. SO, GET YA MIND RIGHT.

TRACK 23

DATE December 16, 2008
ARTIST Plies
ALBUM *Da REALst*
PRODUCED "Plenty Money" and "Watch Dis"

"FOCUS YOUR ENERGY ON DOING WHAT'S IMPORTANT, NOT WHAT'S URGENT."
-DRUMMA BOY

I had the opportunity to collaborate with Plies again on *Da REALst*, which debuted at #1 on Billboard's Top Rap albums chart. While this was his lowest charting album, the single "Plenty Money" was the biggest street song he's ever had in my opinion. What's in my pocket dog, "big face hunnids!"

The thing that made it go was that it was being played on mainstream and urban radio stations, which amplified its reach. And, of course, it was getting crazy spins in clubs across the country. As much as I respect the metrics system's assessment of music, I always look to the culture to see the real value.

The culture can't be compromised, and social currency is powerful. When the beat drops, does it excite the crowd and make them move? Are the people rapping or singing all the words at the shows? I love being on the charts, but data only measures the quantifiable.

I made this beat with the MPC4000 and used live bass and guitar on top of synths I played to give it that timeless sound. You never get tired of hearing live instruments so every now and then I cook up with live bands and creating music for Drumma Boy Live.

Da REALIst is the third studio album from Plies and was released by Atlantic Records. The album debuted at #1 on US *Billboard* Top Rap Albums, and reached #14 on the US *Billboard* 200 and #4 on Top R&B/Hip-Hop Albums. Da REALIst was certified gold by RIAA on June 23, 2016.

D-BOY TALK

I never got into the music industry for the fame. My joy is found strictly in creating music. But as a byproduct of my passion, money has come and also fame. Now, I promoted myself like an artist, and I don't deny that. That's how I built up my name and clientele. People like to work with and stand next to the heat, so I got myself hot. But I want to speak to any of you who are hungry for the attention: just be content with being unknown as long as you can. I'm glad at least I got to experience fame before social media was a thing. When you're in the public's eye, you must constantly "be on," taking your image and behavior into consideration. You don't know who knows you, recording private moments or taking pics without your consent. So be mindful of what you ask for and stay low-key and out of the way as long as you can.

Photo by Robert Underwood

Photo by Grant Mares

TRACK 24

DATE March 17, 2009
ARTIST Gorilla Zoe
ALBUM Don't Feed da Animals
PRODUCED "Lost" featuring Lil Wayne, "I Got It" featuring Big Block, and "Echo"

> "BELIEVING IN YOURSELF IS MAGIC. IF YOU CAN DO THAT, YOU CAN MAKE ANYTHING HAPPEN!"
> —DRUMMA BOY

There were always talks about Jeezy leaving the group Boyz N Da Hood and who would replace him. For someone who didn't even rap before Boyz N Da Hood, Zoe picked up quick watching Yung Joc and was always paying attention. He is one of the most passionate artists that I've worked with. *Don't Feed da Animals*, his second album, an incredible body of work, exemplifies his artistry. The album hit #1 on the *Billboard* Top R&B/Hip-Hop albums chart, and I think it resonated with people because of the narrative.

One night, I was booked for a hosting gig, and Gorilla Zoe happened to be in the club. Soon as my bottles came out, the DJ played "Hood Nigga," and all you saw were sparklers in the air! People stood on couches turning up. He then played "Juice Box," and when you hear groups of people say, "ayyyyyeeeeeeeeeee" when a song first comes on, it's a vibe! These were singles from the first album and his presence was growing. Seeing people's reactions and everybody coming up with their own little dance or popping bottles let me know he had figured out how to make hit records. It was dope seeing Zoe make that introduction as a solo artist and releasing a record without a feature as well as being able to collaborate and hold his own.

On this second album, I produced the leading single, "Lost," that featured Lil Wayne. The lyrics had a depth to them, which touched on mental health issues. Bro tapped into some real emotions that made the music more of an audible experience and engagement between him and his audience. It allowed me to take his sound into an entirely new direction and play to Zoe's strengths.

I slowed up the electronically charged beat that provided the perfect backdrop for him to sing at a low frequency. I experimented with auto-tune without altering the vocal melodies and added big 808 bass sounds meshed with a live baseline and guitar. The song got a lot of love on blogs and from music critics who sometimes don't seem to get rappers who try to step outside the norm of what's trending.

Working with Zoe was fun because I could always present the beats meant for melody, and you could sing too. So many artists wanted trap beats from me, and Gorilla Zoe was open to more of the musical side of me blended with the trap. I think that's why we had so much success with "Lost" because we just poured our emotions into the music and added live instruments. The sound was so different compared to everything out at that time. We went even more pop trap with "I Got It" and "Echo" to push the limits. It's crazy because that sound attracted the likes of Flo Rida and started another amazing relationship.

> *Don't Feed da Animals*, Gorilla Zoe's second studio album, was released on March 17, 2009, and reached #8 on the US *Billboard* 200, #2 on the Top R&B/Hip-Hop Albums, as well as #1 on the *Billboard* Top Rap Albums.

TRACK 24: GLORILLA ZOE

D-BOY TALK

Value your time. Some people don't look at their time as very valuable, but you should. You can tell a lot about a person's respect level for you based on how they treat your time. There are situations beyond your control that can cause you or others to be late, but that should be more of an exception and not the norm. On those occasions when I may be forced to wait, I might read a book on my Kindle app, respond to emails, or return phone calls, but I always try to fill that time with something productive. You can make more money, but you can never make time. Value yours.

Photo by Walter Brady

TRACK 25

DATE April 21, 2009
ARTIST Rick Ross
ALBUM *Deeper Than Rap*
PRODUCED "Face" featuring Trina

> "WHEN YOU PRAY BLESSINGS OVER YOUR LIFE,
> PRAY THOSE SAME BLESSINGS FOR SOMEONE ELSE."
> – DRUMMA BOY

Some artists have a certain work ethic that is attractive and makes you want to work with them. Other artists may have qualities you might dislike or opinions you disagree with. At the end of the day, you gotta get the job done. I've mastered working in noisy environments with lots of people smoking, drinking, and even arguing at this stage in my life. You must be willing to go to any lengths to get the mission accomplished. Once you learn how to capture the moment, you are capable of anything. You will look back and realize that you changed lives with the moments you captured, even your own.

I like to collaborate with those that have a hustler's mentality and about their business. This is how I felt about Ross when I first saw him perform "Hustlin'" in Memphis. His mind frame was always focused on progression and elevation, even seeing how he stepped up his lyricism from the first project to the second. I felt the title of Ross' third album, *Deeper Than Rap*, was introspective because the boss moves he made as well as the ones he is making, are beyond just Hip-Hop. This was Ross' third number-one album, and I produced the track "Face," featuring Trina, one of my favorite female lyricists besides my sister, Gangsta Boo. I like seeing artists working with their hometown talent. As a producer, it helps me create a nostalgic vibe for the city they hail from that brings other people into their world.

Once a project releases and you actually listen for the first time and hear your music on the album, that's when you know it's official. It's like a wave of energy that rotates through the streets, hypnotizing the people. My phone starts ringing like crazy, text messages coming through back-to-back. Everybody's on social media posting from the clubs, home, gym, cars, parties, or wherever, and you have this feeling of accomplishment. I use that burst of energy to make more music and prepare myself for the rush to come. As a businessman, whatever it is that you sale, you want to make sure you keep an inventory of it.

> ***Deeper Than Rap*** **was released on April 21, 2009, via Maybach Music Group (MMG) and Slip-n-slide Records, and distributed by Def Jam Recordings. The album debuted at #1 on the US *Billboard* 200, reached #3 on both the Top R&B/Hip-Hop Albums and Top Rap Albums.**

TRACK 25: RICK ROSS

D-BOY TALK

Educate yourself on what you're trying to do; school yourself. I encourage everybody to read, especially the young people who are just getting into the game, because it's exactly that— a game, and you need to know the rules. If you don't learn the fundamentals, you run the risk of getting played because of your self-inflicted ignorance, which can be a huge waste of your time and other valuable resources. Some rules can be broken or even manipulated, but if you don't know them at their most basic level, you can't even do that.

Photo by: Dominic Fondon

TRACK 26

DATE May 19, 2009
ARTIST DJ Drama
ALBUM Gangsta Grillz The Album Vol. 2
PRODUCED "Day Dreaming" featuring Akon, Snoop Dogg, T.I. and "Gotta Get It" featuring B.G., Juvenile, and Soulja Slim

> "ALWAYS DO YOUR BEST WORK.
> ONE DAY THAT WILL BE YOUR LAST WORK."
> -DRUMMA BOY

My first time ever meeting Snoop Dogg was on the set of DJ Drama's "Day Dreaming" video. I had just touched down in LA and texted Drama like, "What's the address and where da weed at!?"

He said, "When you get here, I will put you on Snoop bus." When I pulled up, I got on the bus, and Drama introduced us. Snoop was like, "Oh, Bet! That beat go hard." He threw an ounce at me and said, "Roll up, *nephew*!" I rolled up the *whole* sack and had at least twenty-two blunts on the table lined up. Unc said, "Damn, nephew, you wasn't playing," and started passing out blunts to everybody who wanted to smoke. I was high as fuck and almost missed my damn cameo. I've lost a lot of loved ones along the way, but I've met some outstanding brothers on that same journey.

Los Angeles is one of those cities that once you get into the matrix, everybody wants to associate with you. That involvement comes with a price attached to it. I always made sure people knew the business before we ever got into the business. That way, everything was understood upfront. That way, you could never have a misunderstanding or a falling out. Communicate, speak your truths or requests, and you'll be surprised what you're granted.

When I first met with Drama a few years prior, he was like, "Bruh, I wish you would have given me some of those beats you gave to some of those underground artists that never saw the light of day." I told him I had some new shit on me right then, and I gave him a beat CD, and he hit my line the next day. "Yo, I just got T.I., Akon, and Snoop on ya shit."

"Day Dreaming" ended up being the first single off of *Gangsta Grillz: The Album Vol. 2*, which featured Akon, Snoop Dogg, and T.I.

I remember being shocked, excited, and proud all at the same time. Akon, T.I., and Snoop were ALL heavyweights in the game, which stamped my name in the game. I kept saying to myself, *what the fuck?* Drama just called me with a play. I was super hype about this major collab, so naturally, I wanted to hear it.

"You're going to hear it," Drama said. "In LA. I need you to get on the flight tonight. We're shooting a video tomorrow."

The next thing I know, Drama booked me a flight and flew me to Cali, and we did the video. I was really amazed at how he just made that happen, and for him to throw the alley-oop like that, I was grateful. Establishing more relationships was essential at that point in my career, and obviously more people wanted to work with me and get music from me. That was the start to me making noise in LA, the west coast, and globally.

Preparing for this trip was easy because I was so excited and made sure I got to the airport earlier than usual. Certain things are hard to live with and missing that flight would have been like blocking a blessing. LA made me feel certified on another level, and I was finally experiencing Hollywood on an intimate level. It's different when you're welcomed everywhere and gaining relationships with the world's top stars.

Gangsta Grillz: The Album Vol. 2 **released on May 19, 2009, by Grand Hustle Records and Atlantic Records and reached #26 on the US *Billboard* 200, #5 on the Top R&B/Hip-Hop Albums, #4 on US Top Rap Albums and #26 on the US Comprehensive Album charts.**

TRACK 26: DJ DRAMA

D-BOY TALK

To be successful at anything in life, you've got to enjoy what you're waking up to do every day. And you've got to be good at it. There've been more years, months, weeks, and days than I can remember where I've gotten less than four hours of sleep, if any, to meet deadlines or just because I was in a creative state of mind and was driven to keep recording.

I'm so passionate about music that I would do it without getting paid. Since I have a natural proclivity for it, the money flows to me. So, get clear on what you would do if money weren't a factor and in something that comes instinctively to you. Then do that every day.

Photo by Zach Wolfe

TRACK 27

DATE September 26, 2009
ARTIST Gucci Mane
ALBUM *The State vs. Radric Davis*
PRODUCED "All About the Money" featuring Rick Ross, "Kush Is My Cologne" featuring Bun B, Devin The Dude, E-40, and "Worst Enemy"

> "INVEST IN YOUR DREAMS AND BANKRUPT YOUR FEARS."
> – DRUMMA BOY

One of the benefits of working with seasoned vets is that they usually know what they want and have a sense of direction when they hit the studio. Both Gucci and Ross are like that. I'm not trying to guess or make assumptions because it's frustrating and a timewaster. Those guys have confidence in themselves and me, so we're able to maximize our efforts out the gate. I like being able to target the sound the artist wants and tailor the beat for an exact fit. When you have this kind of chemistry, the flow is natural. It's always an amazing key factor when an artist is clear and knows what sound they hear for themselves.

On *The State vs. Radric Davis*, there was an equal balance, as the title suggests of music that appealed to the hood and the heart. The mood was decidedly different compared to other Gucci albums, and I wanted to accentuate that theme. He spoke to the flashy side of his flesh on "All About the Money," featuring Ross and "Kush Is My Cologne," featuring Bun B, Devin The Dude, and E-40. At the same time, "Worst Enemy" gave listeners his contemplative side.

One thing about Gucci, he always spoke about what was going on in his life at the time and shared different stories that gave us a different perspective. No matter what he was going through, he always remembered certain things like my phone number by heart or what I liked to eat. Those little things make a difference and create different chemistry that puts extra seasoning on the music.

> *The State vs. Radric Davis* debuted at #10 on the *Billboard* 200 on December 8, 2009, and sold 90,000 copies its first week. The album was certified RIAA Gold on May 31, 2016 and RIAA Platinum certified on July 26, 2023.

D-BOY TALK

Always look for the bigger picture in any situation. It's what I've heard some people phrase as "possibility thinking." You've got to be a little bit of a rebel to get anywhere in this business and world, which is why this kind of thinking is necessary to create new opportunities that lead to growth and out-of-the-box results. Always think of what can be, even though your current situation may reflect a different picture.

Photo by Zach Wolfe

Photo by Lafenye

TRACK 28

DATE October 9, 2009
ARTIST Gucci Mane
ALBUM The Burrprint
PRODUCED "Watch Cost A Bentley," "Yelp, I Got All Of That," "My Shadow," "More" ft Kandi and Sean Ceasar

> *"IN ORDER TO GO UP HIGHER, YOU'RE GOING TO HAVE TO GIVE UP SOMETHING THAT'S HOLDING YOU DOWN."*
> — DRUMMA BOY

Anytime DJ Drama or Gucci Mane hit me, I was pulling up immediately. Gucci Mane was known for doing a mixtape close around the time of dropping an album to give his fans even more material to listen to and have more music to perform on his tours. Most of the beats I did for Gucci would already be cooked up because once Gucci gets to freestyling you want to be able to capture him quickly. He never had too much patience waiting for a beat to be cooked up; he loved when you could just push play and allow him to pick the beat and pull it up.

I would cook-up 10 to 20 beats on my MPC4000 and add some sounds from the triton or Roland keyboard, mix them downright quick and then go pull up on Gucci with the beat CD or hard drive. He was a fan of pianos, horns, and strings so I would always include those sounds in the beats along with that Drumma Boy bounce.

The Burrprint (The Movie 3D) was the final mixtape in Gucci Mane's "The Movie" series. It was hosted by DJ Drama and released on October 9, 2009.

DRUMMA BOY - BEHIND THE HITS

D-BOY TALK

Learn how to turn a product into currency, print your own form of exchange, and always be prepared to market and promote that product.

Photo by Corey Pieper

TRACK 29

DATE November 23, 2009
ARTIST Birdman
ALBUM *Priceless*
PRODUCED "Money To Blow" featuring Drake, Lil Wayne

"IN ORDER TO GO UP HIGHER, YOU'RE GOING TO HAVE TO GIVE UP SOMETHING THAT'S HOLDING YOU DOWN."
— DRUMMA BOY

One afternoon, I got a call from one of my music homies in Canada telling me about this kid from Canada. He kept saying he was on a show named *Degrassi* and that he would be in Atlanta for a few days recording at Hot Beats. I was like, "Cool, let's get it." I'm always excited to collaborate with new artists and put more hits on the wall. "Money To Blow" made me proud because even though Birdman had already released three previous albums and established a name as a rapper, this was the most successful single of his career, which featured Drake and Wayne.

Originally, Drake recorded the hook and his verse, but the rest of the verses were empty. Somehow the session got leaked, and lots of artists got on it at one point with Drake's vocals still on the song. A year later, Birdman calls me out the blue, saying, "I want to purchase the beat for the song Drake did, how much?" I told him my price, and the money was in my bank within thirty minutes. He said, "I'm putting Wayne and Drake on it, then we'll get it mixed." Being able to deliver a smash for another boss CEO, plus Lil Wayne and Drake, was a special moment.

I remember when I heard Drizzy's verse, "Get to shaking something cause that's what Drumma produced it for," that I was going to get a lot more work because of that line. Even as far as I've come in my career, I still appreciate it when the artist shout me out on the beats because it's just another stamp on my work. It feels good to be recognized without asking.

I look at branding like how a label might market its talent. Everything to me is an angle. I always ask myself, how can I maximize this situation that I'm a part of?

I'm sure you're all familiar with the saying, "It's not what you know, but who you know." I; however, prefer to mentally align with the maxim that says, "It's not who you know, but who knows you."

So, with that being said, when an artist mentions your name, whether it's on a track or in an interview, it helps to promote your brand on an amplified level. Whenever and wherever the song or interview is being consumed, your name is getting ingrained into the listener's head. Now, whenever your name is mentioned, people begin to connect dots and know you without you knowing them. That's social currency.

"Money to Blow" ft. Drake and Lil Wayne, was the third single from Birdman's album *Pricele$$*. **"Money To Blow"** was released on November 23, 2009. The single reached #26 on the US *Billboard* Hot 100, #2 on both Hot R&B/Hip-Hop Songs and Hot Rap Songs. "Money to Blow" became RIAA Platinum certified on August 28, 2012.

TRACK 29: BIRDMAN

D-BOY TALK

NETWORK WITH PEOPLE WHO ARE BESIDE YOU. WHENEVER I SPEAK ON PANELS, INEVITABLY, SOMEONE WILL COME UP TO ME WANTING TO CONNECT BY SAYING THEY'RE THE HOTTEST RAPPER, SINGER, VIDEOGRAPHER, PUBLICIST, INFLUENCER, OR DJ OUT. WITHOUT EVEN KNOWING IF THEY'VE GOT THE TALENT OR NOT, I DON'T DISAGREE WITH THEM. INSTEAD, I TELL THEM TO FIND PEOPLE WHO ARE HOT LIKE HOW THEY SAY THEY ARE AND CONNECT WITH THEM. BASICALLY, I'M ENCOURAGING THEM TO ESTABLISH RELATIONSHIPS WITH PEOPLE ON THE SAME LEVEL AS THEY ARE, ALIGN THEIR TALENTS, AND LEVEL UP TOGETHER.

I HAVE SO MANY RELATIONSHIPS WITH PROMINENT ARTISTS NOW BECAUSE I MET THEM WHEN THEY WERE ON THEIR GRIND ALONGSIDE ME. WE SAW THE SAME HUNGER IN ONE ANOTHER, AND AS THE SAYING GOES, "GAME RECOGNIZES GAME." PAY ATTENTION TO THE PEOPLE YOU SEE OUT THERE HUSTLING HARD LIKE YOU AND LINK UP.

TRACK 30

DATE March 13, 2010
ARTIST Gucci Mane
ALBUM *Burrprint 2*
PRODUCED "Intro Live From Fulton County Jail HD," "Boy from the Block," "Gucci On The Rise," "Everybody Looking," "Coca Coca" featuring Rocko, OJ Da Juiceman, Waka Flocka Flame, Shawty Lo, Yo Gotti, Nicki Minaj, "Here We Go Again," "Antisocial," "Beat It Up" featuring Trey Songz, "911 Emergency," "I'm So Tired Of You," "Outro Live from Fulton County Jail HD."

> "IF YOU SAY 'NO' TO HAVING A PLAN, THEN SAY 'YES' TO SUFFERING UNNECESSARY PAIN."
> – DRUMMA BOY

I had the pleasure of producing all but five songs on *Burrprint 2*, which is the follow-up to *The Burrprint* mixtape. There were a ton of high-profile features on this particular project, all of which were done before Gucci went to jail, except for "Intro Live From Fulton County Jail HD," as the title states.

"Beat It Up" with Trey Songz was one of the top-charting singles on the mixtape, and rightfully so, I calibrated it for radio play. Trey's smooth vocals added polish to this street record when combined with Gucci's hood lingo that made for a truly catchy yet classic Hip-Hop record. I wear a lot of different hats in the studio, which includes working in different genres as displayed with this record, skillfully combining R&B with trap.

What I find rather funny is people don't like giving real musicians, like myself, the proper respect we deserve because what we do seems simple. Still, the truth is I make it look effortless because I've done this for over twenty years. I stay learning, growing, pushing myself, asking questions, improving, and investing in myself because I want to always be at my best and deliver my best every single time. I damn near consider the work I did on this mixtape an EP, and it was a blessing to collaborate with the other talented contributors. When you set big goals and work hard to see them come to fruition, it hits differently.

> Gucci Mane's mixtape, *Burrrprint (2) HD*, was released on March 13, 2010, and debuted at #19 on the US *Billboard* 200. *Burrrprint (2) HD* reached #6 on the US Top R&B/Hip Hop Albums and #2 on the Top Rap Albums charts. "Beat It Up" featuring Trey Songs reached #36 on the US *Billboard* Hot R&B/Hip-Hop Songs and #22 on the Rap Song Charts. Music videos were filmed for the songs, "Boy from the Block," "Everybody Looking," "Antisocial" featuring Mylah and "911 Emergency" which debuted at #21 on the Bubbling Under R&B/Hip-Hop Singles chart,

D-BOY TALK

I GREW UP FOLLOWING THE LEGENDARY MOVES OF QUINCY JONES AND DR. DRE; TWO GENIUS PRODUCERS FROM TWO DIFFERENT ERAS. THEY SET THE BAR HIGH, WHICH MAKES ME WANT TO SET IT HIGHER AND LET THAT BE A TREND AMONGST PRODUCERS. SO WE'RE ALL CONTINUOUSLY SHARPENING ONE ANOTHER AND PUTTING OUT QUALITY MUSIC.

I'VE LEARNED SO MUCH BY BEING A STUDENT OF THEIR WORK AND THEIR CREATIVE PROCESSES.

TRACK 30: GUCCI MANE

I had the blessing of meeting Quincy. He invited me to his house once, where several producers who won ASCAP awards attended. We toasted to the hard dedication we served toward our music.

I don't know how many years of my life I've invested in listening to songs they produced to pick up on certain sounds or techniques. I think it's important to have mentors, even if they are ones you don't know personally. In the age of digital media, you have access to a wealth of knowledge via Google. Then there's also the old-fashioned route of picking up and reading a book. Can't afford to buy a book? A library card is free. There is no excuse not to learn. You either want to be successful or you don't— no excuses.

Photo by Father Wolff

TRACK 31

DATE June 8, 2010
ARTIST Lil Jon
ALBUM *Crunk Rock*
PRODUCED "Ms. Chocolate" ft R Kelly & Mario, "Throw It Up" Remix (Part 2) ft Pastor Troy & Waka Flocka Flame, "On de Grind" ft Stephen Marley & Damien Marley

> "BEING PREPARED WHEN OPPORTUNITY PRESENTS ITSELF, WILL CREATE A WORLD OF SUCCESS FOR YOU."
> — DRUMMA BOY

I've been wanting to work with Lil Jon since his King of Crunk days. I remember meeting Lil Jon for the first time when he came to Memphis to work on Yo Gotti's *Life* album. He produced "Dirty South Soldiers" at Slicse Tee's studio off Madison which was downtown in Memphis. Crunk was a memphis term and it was dope seeing him making beats from scratch, learning about our sound and taking crunk to another level. I was excited that I was on an album next to Lil Jon. Gotti's *Life* album opened a lot of doors for all of us.

Working with Lil Jon was a classic moment for me. I never would have thought 8 years later I would be making songs for one of the biggest producers in the south. At the time I was working out of Musichouse Studio in Atlanta previously owned by the producer Shakespeare. Alec Newell and Dru Castro were the new studio owners and had an incredible setup with 3 different studio rooms throughout the house.

One day I was working with Pastor Troy making different beats for a project he was working on and he said "man, Lil Jon would kill this beat." I was like "shit call him & tell him to pull up!" I had no clue he would actually pull up that same day and ended up dropping a hook and a verse. He kept saying "the horns, pianos, & choir voices in this beat are going crazy I need this one for my album." Once Lil Jon did his hook and verse, Pastor Troy dropped his verse and then called Waka Flocka Flame to pull up and get on the record as well.

After we recorded that song Lil Jon said he needed more beats for his album. I'll never forget him telling me how talented I was on the MPC4000 which is still one of my favorite beat machines. That moment helped me land 2 more placements on his album "Ms. Chocolate" ft R Kelly & Mario as well as "On De Grind" ft the legends Stephen & Damien Marley. I couldn't believe I had the opportunity to work with the sons of Bob Marley. This was Lil Jon's 6th overall album which was released by BME and Universal Republic.

> **Lil Jon's Crunk Rock debuted at #49 on the Billboard 200 the week of June 26, 2010.**

TRACK 31: LIL JON

D-BOY TALK

Never be afraid to make a mistake. Accidents are blessings in disguise. My pops would always say if you play a wrong note keep going. Never stop. Those wrong notes sound like diminished chords to the audience which became jazz. The famous jazz musician Miles Davis was known for and made a career out of playing the wrong notes. Don't fear mistakes because there are none!

Photo by Dominic Fondon

TRACK 32

DATE July 20, 2010
ARTIST Usher
ALBUM *Versus*
PRODUCED "Stranger"

> *"DON'T ARGUE WITH UNBELIEVERS.*
> *LET YOUR SUCCESS BE YOUR RESPONSE."*
> —DRUMMA BOY

When Usher or his people call, I'm always there. I enjoy having the opportunity to do work outside of my norm, even though every record I produce is a different experience. I feel incredibly blessed to not only have crossed paths with so many epic artists but to continually get calls to work with them is mind-blowing.

On *Versus*, I produced the record "Stranger" with my boy Dru Castro on the keys and chords. One of the reasons I like crafting R&B/Soul compositions is because you get to appreciate the craftsmanship of the beat along with the storytelling. I can still connect the same with rap, but the difference in the words, sounds, and rhythm are decidedly different. We produced this record at Musichouse studio, which was a dope studio in a mansion that Shakespeare once owned. It was ran by Alec Newell, an engineer, and Dru Castro, a producer engineer. I worked here often for three or four years doing records for B.O.B., Yung Bleu, Rick Ross, and more! The studio just had that vibe and sound for the best musicians, producers, and artists in the game.

This album came about as Usher's marriage was ending, and he was not only single again, but he was also a young father. So, the music just hit differently as a result of that full range of emotions he was feeling.

Being a producer makes me understand how important my role is in the lives of countless people. Many times, the beat dictates the words the artist writes, which places an intangible amount of value in music. When you think about a song's composition from this perspective and the countless ways a record can be interpreted, it's truly a gift from God. *Versus* became Usher's sixth top-ten album and got me my first Grammy.

> Versus, Usher's EP, was released on July 8, 2010 via LaFace Records and Jive Records. The EP peaked at the #4 position on the US Billboard 200 and #3 on US Top R&B/Hip-Hop Albums. It sold over 300,000 copies.

D-BOY TALK

DON'T TAKE SHORTCUTS. WHEN YOU DO, YOU SHORT YOURSELF. MUSIC, PARTICULARLY THE GENRE OF HIP-HOP, GETS A BAD REP FOR ALL SOUNDING THE SAME WITHOUT HAVING A PERSONALITY OR SOUL, NO IMAGINATION OR ORIGINALITY. WHEN YOU TRY TO RECREATE WHAT YOU HEAR ON THE RADIO BECAUSE THAT'S WHAT'S HOT OR IN ORDER TO GET A PLACEMENT, IT WATERS DOWN THE ART OF THE CREATIVE PROCESS OF BEAT MAKING. PUT IN THE NECESSARY TIME TO INVENT SOMETHING THAT SOUNDS LIKE NOTHING ELSE.

Photo by Azn Visuals

TRACK 33

DATE September 28, 2010
ARTIST Gucci Mane
ALBUM *The Appeal: Georgia's Most Wanted*
PRODUCED "What It's Gonna Be" and "Weirdo"

> *"EVERYBODY DOESN'T DESERVE A MINUTE WITH YOU. THEY'LL HAVE YOU RUNNING OUT OF TIME."*
> — DRUMMA BOY

One of the reasons I've been on so many of Gucci's projects is because I have a direct connection with him and all the artists I work with, even though I have a great manager whose been down with me since the early days. I've never relied on just one person to get my music out. Instead, I have a team of people I've developed relationships with over the years who can walk my product through the door.

Don't ever depend on your manager or A&R's, although you want them to represent you. The best position to be in is to have other people working on your behalf, and then you stay out there hustling hard too. You need to come from all angles to get your music circulating to people who can make something happen.

During this time, Gucci was putting out music to feed his fans and also using his unfortunate situation to tell his story. Even though he was locked up, the music unlocked something in him that allowed a rebirth of such to happen in him through his work. The music not only sounded different, but it was also socially different. Listeners were brought into Gucci's world, getting a glimpse of how he was doing mentally through the music.

I contributed two tracks, "What It's Gonna Be" and "Weirdo." These were still considerably classic Gucci records, and I made sure the beats remained rugged as a stamp of authenticity to that fact. These series of projects are definitely like recorded pieces of history because they were created during a challenging time for my friend, but he ended up coming back like a champ. As usual, Gucci made the best usage of his time and talents while away.

> Gucci Mane released his seventh studio album *The Appeal: Georgia's Most Wanted* on September 28, 2019. The album debuted at #4 on the US *Billboard* 200.

D-BOY TALK

STEP OUT OF YOUR COMFORT ZONE AND LEARN TO GET COMFORTABLE WITH BEING UNCOMFORTABLE. MY BIGGEST PAYDAYS HAVE COME FROM DOING SOMETHING OUTSIDE THE BOX OF MY NORMAL DEGREE OF COMFORT. I'VE SAID 'YES' TO ADD ANOTHER THING TO MY PLATE, NOT KNOWING IF I COULD PULL IT OFF BY THE DEADLINE. I'VE DROPPED PROJECTS BEFORE I WAS ALL THE WAY READY. HECK, THIS BOOK IS ME GETTING OUT OF MY COMFORT ZONE, BUT I KNEW IT WOULD BE REWARDING FOR YOU AND ME. I'VE GOTTEN MORE WORK AS THE BYPRODUCT OF CHECK CUTTERS SEEING ME IN A DIFFERENT LIGHT AND DECIDING I WAS SOMEONE WORTH INVESTING IN. YOU CAN'T SWIM AND HOLD ONTO THE EDGE OF THE POOL AT THE SAME TIME. YOU'VE GOT TO TAKE CHANCES TO GROW NOT ONLY YOUR PROFILE BUT ALSO YOUR SELF-CONFIDENCE.

Photo by Walter Brady

Photo by Robert Ector

TRACK 34

DATE October 5, 2010
ARTIST Waka Flocka Flame
ALBUM *Flockaveli*
PRODUCED "No Hands" featuring Roscoe Dash, Wale

> "IF YOU HAVE TO EXPLAIN WHY YOU'RE A 'REAL ONE,' YOU'RE PROBABLY NOT ONE."
> -DRUMMA BOY

Flockaveli was the name of Waka's first album. He'd had massive success with the record "O Let's Do It," which spawned several remixes with notable figures like Diddy, Ross, Wayne, Jeezy, Ludacris, Gucci, and others. I didn't produce it but wanted to mention its success because there were a lot of high expectations attached to everybody involved with his debut. Waka is a character, but he's also smart and understands the game from a street and an industry perspective. He is pure energy, which is part of his value as an artist, and he was aware of his superpowers and used them.

The night we did this record was Gucci Mane's first day out since being locked up for a year. I remember when Waka told me he was going to start rapping when Gucci got locked up again and said he gotta hold down Brick Squad. This was my first time seeing him since he said that to me and had so much success with "O Let's Do It." It was literally a party at Patchwerk Studio celebrating Gucci's release. Every time Gucci gets out of jail he would lock down a studio and knock out music he had written while being incarcerated. I had a beat pack ready for Gucci as he was working in the A room and I knew he would be ready to work.

While he was in the booth recording "First Day Out" and "Abnormal," I went into the B room where my equipment was setup and Waka, Roscoe, Wale, Rici, and plenty of people were hanging out. I started cooking up the "No Hands" beat while everyone was really just talking and I could see Roscoe was really vibing with the beat so I told him to go in the booth if he had something ready. The first words that came out of his mouth was "Girl, drop it to the floor I love the way your booty go," and the whole room LIT UP! Next thing you know, Waka was hype like, "Yo, I got something for this," and Wale rapped it up with his contributions! Who knew we would have one of the biggest anthems for the ladies and the clubs!

I wanted to make a song that had the same kind of rambunctiousness that is the force known as Waka, and I made it my job to add to his gift. I wanted to craft a fun and catchy record to drive people to the dance floor, but that also has a hard-hitting edge to it. Waka is a cool guy, but he's also got a hood element to him, and I didn't want to dilute that part of his character. I added drama to the track through a sonic progression of intense horns and bass. I also believe Roscoe and Wale's collaborative combinations were an unlikely match, but the chemistry was flawless. The record went triple platinum, won the BET Hip-Hop award for Best Club Banger in 2011, and hit #1 on the *Billboard* Hot Rap Songs chart when it was released.

Waka Flocka Flame released "No Hands" featuring Roscoe Dash and Wale from his debut studio album *Flockaveli*. The single was released on August 17, 2010, debuting on the US *Billboard* Hot 100 at #45 but climbing to its peak position at #13. "No Hands" peaked at #1 on the Hot Rap Songs chart, #2 on Hot R&B/Hip-Hop Songs, and it reached #3 on the Rhythmic chart as well appeared as high as #28 on the Mainstream Top 40. In 2023 "No Hands" was certified RIAA Diamond.

***Flockaveli* was released on October 5, 2010 via Asylum Records and the album debuted at #6 on the US *Billboard* 200.**

TRACK 34: WAKA FLOCKA FLAME

D-BOY TALK

Everybody wants to be so hard. Still, a lot of people don't realize how imperative it is to have a genuine excitement about what you're doing. The late great Nipsey Hussle once said that the way you keep your fans excited is for you to be and stay excited about what you're working on. I've listened to and seen a lot of interviews with entertainers over the years. There've been times when I couldn't believe how nonchalant these people were about what they were promoting. Put some respect on your art and be excited about it. If you're not passionate about the work you're doing, you may need to reevaluate your goals.

TRACK 35

DATE October 31, 2010
ARTIST Young Buck
ALBUMS *Back on My Buck Shit Vol. 2: Change of Plans*, *B.O.M.B.S vol. 3*, and *Live Loyal, Die Rich*
PRODUCED Entire Mixtapes

> *"IF YOU CALL A MAN YOUR TRUE HOMIE, YOU'RE GOING TO BE DOWN THROUGH GOOD TIMES AND WHEN SHIT HITS THE FAN!"*
> —DRUMMA BOY

Let me tell you something, me and Young Buck go way back. He's what I consider my 'Day 1.' I don't turn my back on my people no matter what the situation is. Buck had a lot of success with G-Unit, but by 2010 he was making a comeback. Buck was going through some trying times; we all heard about the tranny fiasco. Listen, I knew this man my whole life and I can say for sure that Buck isn't gay. That's on facts!

When I was producing *Back on My Buck Shit Vol. 2*, I went at it with the eye of the fucking tiger! I felt like Buck was the underdog, and I was going to make him a top dog again with this mixtape. And just like the energy I put into it, it was a huge success! Buck downloaded 50,000 times in less than a month! My boy was back on the scene.

That mixtape is a classic! It was such a success that we recorded vol. 3 shortly after vol. 2, and again it did phenomenal numbers. Young Buck was back, and he was going full steam ahead with his newfound success. Off of vol. 2 and 3, Young Buck was able to secure a decent deal and make some money, and that is what's most important in this industry.

Me and Young Buck were on a roll, so we didn't stop there. I produced *Live Loyal, Die Rich* and of course it was another banger. It meant a lot to me to see my brother get back on top after everyone counted him out. The grind was real! I watched Buck shoot straight to the top, then fall off, then get back on, in the blink of an eye. That's what I call persistence because he could've given up like most artists from his time. Not many rappers from 2005 had Buck's career.

On top of that, the hottest producers of today have approached me and admitted that the production I did on Young Buck's mixtapes inspired their sound. I'm talking about monumental producers like Metro Booming, London on da Track, and Tay Keith just to name a few. This is just proof that when you do things from the heart the outcome will always be great.

> **Young Buck released *Back on My Buck Shit Vol. 2: Change of Plans* on October 31, 2010. He dropped Live Loyal Die Rich, another mixtape featuring appearances by The Outlawz and All Star Cashville Prince, on January 24, 2012. Both mixtapes were hosted by Drumma Boy, the latter being hosted along with DJ Crisis.**

TRACK 35: YOUNG BUCK

D-BOY TALK

THE BETTER WE COMMUNICATE THE MORE EFFECTIVE WE BECOME. PRACTICE THE ABILITY TO HEAR WHAT ISN'T SAID. ONCE I MASTERED THIS, I WAS ABLE TO CHANGE LIVES. I LEARNED HOW TO DELIVER WHAT WAS MISSING. THE CIRCLE IS SMALLER BUT INCLUDES LESS GOSSIP AND MORE ENCOURAGEMENT. LESS PAST, MORE PRESENT & FUTURE. LESS TOXICITY, MORE POSITIVITY. STARVE YOUR DISTRACTIONS AND FEED YOUR FOCUS!

TRACK 36

DATE April 29, 2011
ARTIST Musiq Soulchild
ALBUMS *MusiqInTheMagic*
PRODUCED "Waitingstill" with Jerry Wonda

> *"THOSE WHO OVERINDULGE TEND TO OVERDOSE."*
> — DRUMMA BOY

I'm definitely a Hip-Hop head, but I also stay in-tune with other genres like jazz, classical, soul, gospel, indie rock, and R&B. Many times, I'll become inspired by listening to all sorts of music and will get a melody in my head, hum it out, and then make the beat based off that. That's how I started the process with "Waitingstill" for Musiq Soulchild on his sixth album, *MusiqInTheMagic*.

I took into account his signature soft sound. Still, I wanted to also add my sauce because otherwise, what's the point in bringing a producer like me to the table. At least that's how I look at cross-genre collabs. I also have writing credits on this track, which can happen unexpectedly when structuring a record.

There is no one path when it comes to songwriting. Inspiration flows in various directions and can bring about hidden gems you never conceived. That's why I champion the collaborative process because when everybody's vibing in the same space, magic is bound to happen. Or, as Mr. Quincy Jones has said, *'Leave space for God to walk into the room.'* That's the only way I can define that experience; it's supernatural and inexplicable.

Be confident in your abilities and talents but humble enough to know that you don't know it all. Along with Jerry and a few others, we created a beautiful piece of work that I'll always be proud of. Having that feeling is more important than money. You can always hustle up on a check, but to take the utmost pride in your work and actually mean it, that's priceless.

> *MusiqInTheMagiq* was released on April 29, 2011 and was Musiq Soulchilds sixth studio album. The album made it to #8 on US *Billboard* 200 and #3 on the US Top R&B/Hip-Hop Albums.

D-BOY TALK

STAY PREPARED AT ALL TIMES SO THAT WHEN YOUR OPPORTUNITY HITS, NOT ONLY WILL YOU RECOGNIZE IT, BUT YOU CAN ALSO SEIZE IT. THERE'S NOTHING MORE PITIFUL THAN TO WATCH SOMEBODY WHO HAS THE TALENT BUT LACKS THE HUSTLE TO TAKE ADVANTAGE OF LIFE-ALTERING OPPORTUNITIES.

WHEN I HEAR YOUNG PRODUCERS OR OTHER CREATIVE ENTREPRENEURS TELL ME THEY'RE READY FOR THEIR BIG BREAK, I RESPOND BY ASKING THEM QUESTIONS. I ASK THEM IF THEY HAVE AN ATTORNEY ON DECK FOR CONTRACTS OR TO GET LEGAL ADVICE? DO THEY KEEP A FLASH DRIVE OF BEATS ON THEM AT ALL TIMES? EVEN IF THEY'RE JUST HEADED TO THE GROCERY STORE. DO THEY HAVE A LITTLE CASH SAVED UP

TRACK 36: MUSIQ SOULCHILD

IN CASE THEY NEED TO BOOK STUDIO TIME, CATCH A FLIGHT, OR GAS UP THE CAR TO MAKE SOMETHING HAPPEN? I ASK THEM IF THEY HAVE A BIO OR AN EPK—ELECTRONIC PRESS KIT OR EVEN A WEBSITE SET UP. THOSE SIMPLE CONCEPTS ARE USUALLY FOREIGN TO THEM.

INSTEAD OF COMPLAINING OR WAITING, GET PREPARED FOR ALL SCENARIOS SO THAT WHEN YOUR HARD WORK MEETS OPPORTUNITY, YOU'LL BE READY TO TAKE OFF BOTH FIGURATIVELY AND LITERALLY.

Photo by Thomas Jacobi

TRACK 37

DATE June 14, 2011
ARTIST Gorilla Zoe
ALBUMS *King Kong*
PRODUCED "King Kong," "Party Over Here"

> "SEEK RESPECT, NOT REVENGE."
> —DRUMMA BOY

I teamed back up with Zoe on *King Kong*, his third album because I respect him as an artist and a man. He's proven repeatedly that he gives his all and pours it into his art. I also like building beats around his unique gruff voice. Being that I'm one of those self-assured producers who believes he can turn any artist's career around, especially a dope one, I like to roll the dice.

However, sometimes the music just doesn't connect and meet the audience's demands. Perhaps the audience is there but has adopted a new artist to champion. It can be a number of things, and I'm not sure why Zoe didn't regain his proper status, but the two songs I produced on this particular project were hard-hitting yet straightforward.

The title track "King Kong" had a bit of a pop-rock vibe with electric guitars, while I fleshed out the structure of "Party Over Here," adding in a lot of hi-hats and snares. Zoe went back to his original G-talk on *King Kong* after having put out a previous body of work that was predominantly self-reflective and kind of dark.

These new tracks were the complete opposite— more upbeat, fun, and club friendly. I think we inspired each other and brought futuristic sounds and classic hood anthems together that will go down as some of our greatest artistic achievements.

> Gorilla Zoe dropped his third album, *King Kong* on June 14, 2011. The album debuted at #56 on the US *Billboard* 200, and reached #12 Top R&B/Hip-Hop Albums as well as #8 Top Rap Albums.

D-BOY TALK

Once you make a powerful decision, live and die by that decision. I'm from the old school of thought where you don't switch up when things get hard or when they don't go as you predicted. Avoid the pitfall of choosing the easy route that any and everybody takes to get any and everybody's results. We were all born with greatness in us; don't die without emptying yours to the benefit of yourself and others.

Photo by Dominic Fondon

TRACK 38

DATE October 11, 2011
ARTIST DJ Drama
ALBUMS *Third Power*
PRODUCED "Oh My" featuring Fabulous, Roscoe Dash, Wiz Khalifa, "Me and My Money" featuring Gucci Mane, and "Oh My" (remix) featuring Trey Songz, 2Chainz, Big Sean

> *"I CAN TELL A LOT ABOUT A PERSON WHO DOESN'T CONSIDER HIS LEGACY."*
> — DRUMMA BOY

No matter how many times I've worked with the same artist, my goal is to always come with a new sound. One way I do this is by exposing my eyes and ears to something opposite of what I normally would. I may watch a foreign film, listen to world music, or get a hotel room on a different side of town and submerse myself in things exclusive to that area. I'm guaranteed to catch a vibe and put that feeling into the music.

I enjoy the privilege of repeatedly working with good people like Drama; he's a real music guy. Obviously, as a DJ, he has an excellent ear for a song's technical aspect, but he also knows a hit when he hears one. It makes the collaborative process challenging in a good way because he is such a sharp guy. It keeps me on my toes since I know he understands the anatomy of production. I think you can hear when the artist/producer chemistry is solid; it elevates the music's quality, and the listener gets a chance to feel that creative energy.

"Oh My" was the lead single from Drama's third album entitled *Third Power*. With Fab from up top, Roscoe from down bottom, and Wiz hailing from the east coast made for a lyrical gumbo that complemented every Hip-Hop taste bud. The streets spoke on this record too because it grabbed the #1 spot on the *Billboard* Hot 100 chart when it debuted, and it also became Drama's first intro on the chart.

I want to point out the obvious by emphasizing that this was my dawg's first time hitting the chart, but it was also his third project. Sometimes success happens instantly, but it's usually a brick-by-brick method where you build the house over time, not overnight.

This single also peaked at #1 on the *Billboard* Hot R&B/Hip-Hop Songs chart and #12 on the Hot Rap Songs chart, which became his highest-charting song on both of those charts. It's always annoying and frustrating when people doubt you. Still, if you lay a solid foundation and stay solid with people as well as to your craft, your results will speak on your behalf. Numbers don't ever lie.

"Oh My," the lead single from DJ Drama's album, *Third Power*, was released on June 17, 2011, and features Fabolous, Wiz Khalifa, and Roscoe Dash. It entered the US *Billboard* 100 at position 100 and peaked at #95. The single reached #18 at Hot R&B /Hip Hop Songs, #12 on the Hot Rap Songs and #1 Bubbling Under Hot 100.

Third Power was released on October 11, 2011 and reached #42 on the US *Billboard* 200, #7 on the Top R&B/Hip Hop Albums and on the US Independent Albums charts. It also reached #6 on the Top Rap Albums Chart.

TRACK 38: DJ DRAMA

D-BOY TALK

WHEN YOU CAN'T SEE YOUR WAY, KEEP WORKING. WHEN YOU WANT TO THROW EVERYTHING AWAY BECAUSE WHAT YOU'RE RECEIVING ISN'T MATCHING THE AMOUNT OF EFFORT YOU'RE PUTTING IN, KEEP WORKING. WHEN NOBODY IS TAKING A CHANCE ON YOU WHEN NOBODY IS RETURNING YOUR CALLS OR EMAILS, WHEN YOU HAVE MONEY CHALLENGES OR FAMILY ISSUES, KEEP WORKING. IF YOU DON'T GIVE UP ON YOURSELF, YOU WILL WIN IN DUE TIME.

TRACK 39

DATE October 25, 2011
ARTIST Goapele
ALBUMS *Break of Dawn*
PRODUCED "Right Here"

> "SOME OF YOUR BIGGEST CHALLENGES YOU WILL HAVE TO FACE ALONE. STAY PREPARED."
> —DRUMMA BOY

I established a professional relationship with the Bay's own Goapele through a former publicist, Sasha Brookner, I was working with at the time. I was already a fan of her music and recognized her talent the instant I heard her sing. One of my favorite records she did was "Closer." It was soulful, sensual, and sexy, but that 808 pulsating throughout gave the record some street texture. Her voice sounded like a poetry set to music to me. In fact, you could actually categorize her voice as an instrument itself. So, I was eager to complement what I did best with her voice's soulfulness. I knew she was the kind of artist that no matter what beat I crafted, it wouldn't take away from the emotions she would express.

I produced "Right Here," a love song on her album *Break of Dawn*, which is a feel-good song about being happy right where you are with whoever that special someone is for you. When we first met, she let me hear some of the vibes from the project, and the only thing missing to me was a trap bounce with a mix of major key progressions. I presented her with a few options, and we got to work! It was an amazing feeling being able to bring out exactly what she wanted to express. To me, that's what great producers do.

At this time in my career, I had just won a Grammy with Usher for "Stranger," and "No Hands" for Waka was huge! But after a while, burnout developed. I still loved what I was doing and the artists I was doing it with, but everything started to sound the same, and I needed some fresh inspiration. Working with Usher, Goapele, Jagged Edge, and other R&B artists allowed me to express more of the musician side I'm so passionate about. I never lost that drive or enthusiasm I had for making beats when I was a kid, but I felt empty like I'd done it all before. We all get writer's block at times and having an alternative music genre to work helped me roll over this artistic speed bump. The melody on this particular single was strong and triumphant, as were the lyrics.

> **Goapele released *Break of Dawn* after a five-year hiatus on October 25, 2011. Three singles from the album were released including, "Right Here," produced by Drumma Boy.**

TRACK 39: GOAPELE

D-BOY TALK

NOT ACTING ON YOUR GOALS IS A COSTLY MISTAKE, AND YET PEOPLE STILL KEEP PAYING THE PRICE. EVERY DAY YOU SHOULD PLANT A SEED. AND WHILE THAT SEED MIGHT NOT LOOK OR FEEL LIKE MUCH, YOU'RE INVESTING IN YOUR FUTURE. THE MOST EXCITING PART ABOUT THIS METHOD OF WORKING IS THAT YOU NEVER KNOW WHEN THE FRUITS OF YOUR LABOR WILL MATERIALIZE. ANY DAY COULD BE THE DAY YOU REAP ONE OR MULTIPLE BENEFITS. STAY FOCUSED AND EMBRACE THE PROCESS OF PLANTING.

Photo by Dee Lenz

TRACK 40

DATE December 13, 2011
ARTIST Snoop Dogg and Wiz Khalifa
ALBUMS *Mac & Devin Go to High School*
PRODUCED "Smokin' On" featuring Juicy J

> *"IF YOU MASTER THE ART OF COMMUNICATION, YOU CAN DO ANYTHING."*
> —DRUMMA BOY

This is one of my favorite collaborative projects between an OG, Snoop Dogg, and young OG, Wiz Khalifa. To be a part of this project was another classic moment for me and a no-brainer for me as far as a topic. It was for the soundtrack to a film they did together, *Mac & Devin Go to High School*. "Young, Wild & Free," featuring Bruno Mars, was the most popular song from the album and was successful worldwide.

Instead of going straight into the studio like I usually do to create something, I approached this record from the perspective of a fan of Snoop, Wiz, and Juicy J. I also immersed myself in a smoker's atmosphere, which wasn't really against the grain since that's the typical environment for me. Still, I wanted to re-create the feeling of being in an outdoor arena that everybody could smoke in. A feeling like Coachella or Memphis In May music festival and everybody in the crowd is repeating the words and smoking on the best strains of weed!

My first time working with Wiz Khalifa was at 11th Street Studio when he was in Atlanta on a promo for "Black And Yellow" in 2010. Being familiar with an artist always helps the chemistry of the session because you know how to cater to them. Since I was familiar with Wiz and Snoop, it was easy for me to make music tailor made for them.

Mac & Devin Go to High School is the soundtrack to the film "Mac & Devin Go to High School" starring Snoop Dogg and Wiz Khalifa. The soundtrack was released December 13, 2011 reaching #29 on the US *Billboard* 200, #6 on the Top R&B/Hip-Hop Albums, #3 on the Top Rap Album and #3 on US Soundtrack Albums. *Mac & Devin Go to High School* was certified gold by the RIAA on July 14, 2016.

"Smokin' On," a record from the soundtrack featuring Juicy J, reached #17 on US *Billboard* Bubbling Under Hot 100 singles and #23 on Rap Digital Song Sales.

D-BOY TALK

MY GRANDFATHER WAS ONE OF MY BIGGEST SUPPORTERS. I'M SURE THERE WERE TIMES HE THOUGHT I WAS CHASING A PIPE DREAM, AND HE DIDN'T FULLY UNDERSTAND MY VISION, BUT THAT DIDN'T STOP HIM FROM SPEAKING ENCOURAGING WORDS TO ME.

HE'D SAY SOME STUFF LIKE, "KEEP, KEEP DOING YA MUSIC, JUST KEEP DOING YA MUSIC," AND JUST THAT SIMPLE PHRASE WOULD ALTER MY ENTIRE DAY. I'M NOT EVEN CERTAIN HE UNDERSTOOD HOW THE WEIGHT AND POWER OF THOSE WORDS POSITIVELY AFFECTED ME.

I'M TELLING Y'ALL THIS BECAUSE THAT CAN BE ENCOURAGING TO THE HOMIES WHO ARE OUT HERE TRYING TO PUT THEIR ART OUT INTO THE WORLD. YOU NEVER KNOW WHAT A SIMPLE "KEEP DOING YA THANG" CAN MEAN TO SOMEBODY

TRACK 40: SNOOP DOGG AND WIZ KHALIFA

WHO MAY NOT HAVE A FRIEND OR FAMILY MEMBER ROOTING FOR THEM. IT'S ALL ABOUT PUTTING GOOD ENERGY OUT THERE, MAN, AND YOU'LL RECEIVE BACK WHATEVER YOU GIVE OUT.

TRACK 41

DATE December 20, 2011
ARTIST Young Jeezy
ALBUMS *Thug Motivation 103 Hustlerz Ambition*
PRODUCED "What It Do (Just Like That)," featuring Bun B and "Lose My Mind" featuring Plies

"IF YOU SAY YOU'RE GOING TO DO SOMETHING, JUST DO IT."
—DRUMMA BOY

Getting back in the studio with Jeezy is always like a family reunion. This was a highly anticipated project since this album was a sequel in the *Thug Motivation* series. I think people took heed to my music after I did "Standing Ovation" for *TM 101*, honestly. Since I'm a musician, I really make good music, and good music will always be listened to; good music will always be supported and will always prevail.

Dope records are going to forever be heard, and I think I understood that at an early age, and people kind of gravitated toward young ones like me who took their craft seriously. It's like Steph Curry. You look at the success he's had over the years; he's an amazing ball-handler as well as an amazing shooter. If you look at how he moves when he doesn't have the ball in his hands, he's running off screens, going through and around picks, calling plays— all those things that you don't pay attention to. It makes him a triple threat, and that's what I feel like; I'm a triple threat as far as music theory, versatility, and artist ability. You must be a therapist with the artist and dive into their world to deliver the results for them on the beats. The more questions you ask an artist, the better you can see the picture that you are trying to express.

I think it's important for creative entrepreneurs to cater to the will of the artist without losing their personal identity. I know different combinations make people great, and for me, being able to play multiple positions was something I was doing from an early age. When I mentioned earlier on in this book that I was given the challenge to come up with a harder beat than the original one Jeezy wanted, and in less than twenty-four hours, I tapped into those back-against-the-wall emotions and did my thing. He didn't believe I was going to be able to top that old beat, but I did, and that's why he fucks with a nigga so heavy.

On *Thug Motivation 103: Hustlerz Ambition*, which was nominated for Best Rap Performance By Duo or Group at the 2011 Grammy's, I worked my magic on the lead single, "Lose My Mind," featuring Plies. I feel like I got back to the basics with the aggressive synth lines and severe 808 snares, which was even more pronounced with both Jeezy and Plies lyrical delivery. "What It Do" was a classic collab— straight raw energy and solid drums. Some music you can't appreciate unless you hear it loud in a studio or a club, and I think this is one of those records. It's powerful and takes me back to the early days when I first started working with Jeezy.

To this day, when "Lose My Mind" comes on, people recite it word for word with energy like it dropped last week. Making music is a gift in itself but seeing how far my music travels and how much people appreciate it years later, gives me the feeling of a king. I've always aimed to make timeless music, and to see it manifest is a blessing.

TM: 103 Hustlerz Ambition released on December 20, 2011, with its lead single "Lose My Mind" featuring Plies. The single peaked at #35 on the *Billboard* Hot 100, #5 on the Hot R&B/Hip-Hop Songs and #3 on Hot Rap Songs. "Lose My Mind" was nominated for Best Rap Performance by a Duo or Group at the 53rd Annual Grammy Awards. The song is certified platinum by the RIAA for selling over a million copies.

TM: 103 Hustlerz Ambition sold 233,000 copies its first week out, it was certified gold a month later and in 2020, RIAA certified the album platinum. The album peaked at #3 on the *Billboard* 200 and #1 on the Top R&B/Hip-Hop Albums.

TRACK 41: YOUNG JEEZY

D-BOY TALK

Grinding is really about how hard you want it and your character. If you've been in enough challenging situations where you ain't never had shit when you do get something, you'll appreciate it.

And that's why I never fall as opposed to people who have had shit all their life; they ain't really appreciating it. The next guy might be more famous than me. They might be richer or whatever. But is he happy with his life?

I'd rather have two to three million in my bank and be happy as fuck and speak passionately every day than to have 50-100 million living alone and sleeping with a different woman every night. It may sound funny, but you should want to start building on some real shit and not on stuff that's fleeting.

Photo by Hannibal Matthews

TRACK 42

DATE February 5, 2012
ARTIST Gucci Mane
ALBUMS *Trap Back*
PRODUCED "Thank You," "Sometimes" featuring Future

> "A STAND-UP REPUTATION IS WORTH MORE THAN MONEY."
> -DRUMMA BOY

If Gucci is nothing else, he's consistent and stays down, which is why I'm always glad to cook up whenever he's working on something. Gucci knows my number by heart, so when he calls, I know it's about some work or an invite to something special. We know we are a dynamic duo, and in both of these songs, Gucci references more commas each time we connect.

Trap Back was a mixtape that was certified 2x platinum hosted by DJ Holiday and was downloaded over 800,000 times on Datpiff. During this time, dropping music for free was the wave for an artist because it got them hot in the streets, and they would feast off shows. A lot of people don't see the value in releasing mixtapes these days. However, I think they are still very relevant for an artist to be discovered and create their fan base. With all of Gucci's legal problems throughout the years, doing mixtapes helped to keep his voice, likeness, and brand alive until he got back on point.

I put my stamp on "Thank You" and "Sometimes" featuring Future. When people hear me say, "Aye Yeaahhh Boyyyy," they know it's official, and the song is about to go hard. I feel like this could've been an actual album because it was nothing but solid tracks backed by A-1 artists and a respected list of production talent, which raised the project's quality level. The project did these numbers with no promo or support. So, I can only imagine how bigger it could've been with a label push behind it. Anytime you have 2 Chainz, Rocko, Yo Gotti, Jadakiss, Future, Waka Flocka, Sonny Digital, Mike Will, Lex Lugar, Zaytoven, Fatboi, and Drumma Boy on one album, it's a problem!

> Trap Back, Gucci Mane's mixtape was released on February 5, 2012 at 10:17am and reached "2x Platinum" status on the mixtape site, Datpiff, with more than 500,000 downloads.

D-BOY TALK

YOU HAVE TO EDUCATE YOURSELF. THERE'S NO REASON YOU SHOULD BE FAILING IN THIS LIFE WITH TECHNOLOGY. YOU CAN GO ON THE INTERNET AND FIND ANY ANSWER YOU WANT TO FIND. YOU CAN ASK SIRI, AND SIRI HAS MORE BRAINS THAN SOME OF THESE CATS OUT HERE. TRY READING SOMETHING. I READ AS MUCH AS I CAN, PARTICULARLY ON THOSE INDIVIDUALS I LOOKED UP TO OR THOSE WHO HAD SOME SORT OF INFLUENCE ON MY LIFE, ESPECIALLY IF THEY HAVE AN AUTOBIOGRAPHY.

Photo by Azn Visuals

Photo by Robert Ector

TRACK 43

DATE August 14, 2012
ARTIST 2 Chainz
ALBUMS *Based on a T.R.U. Story*
PRODUCED "Money Machine"

> "CHEMISTRY DOESN'T COME WITH A MANUAL. IT JUST FLOWS."
> -DRUMMA BOY

I go back with 2 Chainz when he was rapping by the name of Tity Boi, and I was pulling up on him at his grandmother's house playing beats and dropping off CDs. It was always cool linking up with him because he would freestyle over beats and entertain me for hours. From the beginning, I knew he would evolve into one of the world's biggest artists. Whenever we bumped into each other, it was always a genuine vibe, and we grew from that. I came through for 2 Chainz in the clutch with records like "Boo," and Spend It" on *TRU Religion*, and he made sure I was on his first solo project, *Based On A T.R.U Story*. It's always appreciated when an artist shows his loyalty to you, and I respect that.

Everybody knows 2 Chainz has always had talent. He's been super lyrical, and his verses are also entertaining— that's a major key. Whenever you hear him rhyme, it makes you want to be around him because you want to have that same energy; you want to hear that next verse, that next line. I knew we'd connect again eventually, and it's certain beats I would hold because I could hear him going crazy on them. Anytime I make a beat, I feel like it can help the artist express how they feel at that moment.

When I first made the beat, I was thinking about cartoon sounds and how I could match 2 Chainz's lyrical ability with his comical punchline side as well. It usually takes about five to ten minutes to make the beat, and then I start to perfect that particular vibe. Sometimes I create concepts or hooks depending on if the artist is open to ideas. 2 Chainz immediately started rapping to the beat, and when he likes something, he usually finishes the song pretty quickly. It's crazy. I was just happy to make the album, but I had no clue it would end up getting a Grammy nod for Best Rap Album.

> On August 14, 2012, 2 Chainz released his debut studio album *Based on a T.R.U. Story* on Def Jam Recordings. The album was nominated for Best Rap Album at the 55th Grammy Awards. The album sold 147,000 copies its first week and debuted at #1 on the US *Billboard* 200. It peaked at #1 on both Top R&B/Hip-Hop Albums and Top Rap Albums charts. *Based on a T.R.U. Story* was certified gold December 2012 by the RIAA and ultimately certified platinum for selling over a million copies on March 29, 2016.

D-BOY TALK

My mom was a warehouse manager and accounting specialist for a company that produced car parts for NASCAR. I get a lot of my business mindset from her and also my grandmother. She was an entrepreneur and created her own currency. The same thing can be said about my aunt, who did hair, and my brother, who was a barber in addition to making beats.

TRACK 43: 2 CHAINZ

DIFFERENT FAMILY MEMBERS MOTIVATED ME JUST AS FAR AS GETTING TO IT AND CREATING OPPORTUNITIES TO EARN A LIVING. WHENEVER I'D GO TO ANY OF THEM AS A KID FOR MONEY, THEY'D BASICALLY TELL ME TO GO EARN IT. AND THEY WEREN'T WITH JUST HANDING OUT BREAD BECAUSE I ASKED. AFTER I UNDERSTOOD THAT APPROACH WASN'T GOING TO FLY WITH THEM, I LEARNED HOW TO EARN AN INCOME ON MY OWN.

I TELL THAT STORY TO ENCOURAGE YOU TO NOT ONLY FIND A LEGITIMATE WAY TO MAKE A LIVING, BUT TO ESTABLISH SEVERAL WAYS TO HAVE CHECKS COMING IN SO YOU'LL NEVER HAVE TO RELY ON A SINGLE SOURCE. YOU DON'T WANT YOUR LIFESTYLE TO BE ALTERED BECAUSE OF SOMEONE ELSE'S DECISION OR LACK THEREOF. GROWING UP HOW I DID MADE ME HUSTLE AND NOT WAIT OR DEPEND ON ANYBODY BECAUSE THAT MEANT OTHER PEOPLE HAD CONTROL OVER ME. I NEVER WANTED TO BE THAT GUY, AND BY THE GRACE OF GOD, I HAVEN'T HAD TO BE. AND ONE FINAL THING, DON'T BE IGNORANT OF BUDGETS AND THE BUSINESS SIDE OF MUSIC. THE KNOWLEDGE IS OUT THERE.

Photo by Walter Brady

TRACK 44

DATE December 4, 2012
ARTIST Wiz Khalifa
ALBUMS O.N.I.F.C.
PRODUCED "Bluffin" featuring Berner and "It's Nothin" featuring 2 Chainz

> "LIFE WILL GIVE YOU WHATEVER EXPERIENCE IS MOST HELPFUL FOR THE EVOLUTION OF YOUR CONSCIOUSNESS. STAY WOKE!"
> —DRUMMA BOY

Writing this book has made me recall my experiences with these artists. I've recognized a recurring theme in most of them, which is an overwhelming self-confidence in what they're doing.

Wiz and I connected on that vibe a few years before this album, in addition to his having a grand vision for himself. He believed he was dope before the masses did. I can relate to that ambition; the key in the success formula is self-belief.

One of the things I love about working with Wiz is that he's just as much a pop and rockstar as he is a rapper, and rightfully so. His music influences diverse groups of people outside of Hip-Hop culture. He's cultivated a legion of supporters by doing him. It's that rebellious spirit and disruptive brashness that I like to put into the music because it's authentically Wiz.

The first sound I used when I made the beat for "Bluffin" was the conga drums. I wanted it to feel like a chill vibe that you could ride around and smoke to. I added the chords and 808, and the rest was history. Once I figure out an artists' style and what type of beats they like, it gets dangerous. I can even hear what key certain artists' voices sound good on and blend with the music.

Once the beat was loaded, Wiz put it on loop and just started writing in his head for about ten to twenty minutes before he went into the booth to record. I feel like the intro was longer than usual because he talked over the first hook section, but we flipped it and put "I Got So Much" chop from the original hook on top before his first verse. After he dropped his second verse, Berner goes in and puts the perfect addition to the breakdown at the end.

As a producer, it's important to take into consideration whom you're working with. Even though there will be times you will be tasked with pushing creative boundaries with the artist and for yourself (as you should), you still have to preserve the DNA of the artist in the music.

Being in the studio with Wiz is always a room full of smoke, drinks, and good music. It's almost like a peaceful party, and you forget where you really are. Often, when I'm in the studio, I feel like I'm in a spaceship making music for light years to come. When the vibes are crazy, it could be 8 or 9 A.M. before we end a session.

> **O.N.I.F.C. released by Wiz Khalifa on December 4, 2012, on Atlantic and Rostrum Records. The album debuted at #2 on the US *Billboard* 200 and reached #1 on the US Top R&B/Hip Hop Albums and touched the *Billboard* charts in nine other countries. O.N.I.F.C. was certified RIAA Gold and Platinum on June 20, 2016.**

TRACK 44: WIZ KHALIFA

D-BOY TALK

IN ORDER TO MOVE FORWARD, YOU'VE GOT TO STOP LOOKING BACK. SO, STOP REFLECTING ON WHAT DIDN'T WORK, WHO DIDN'T SUPPORT, HOW THE DEAL FELL THROUGH, OR WHY YOU HAVEN'T GOTTEN THE BIG OPPORTUNITY.

WORRYING AND GETTING WORKED UP ABOUT THINGS THAT HAVE ALREADY HAPPENED IS ROBBING YOU OF FOCUSING YOUR ENERGIES TOWARD MAKING WORTHWHILE ACCOMPLISHMENTS.

REFLECT JUST LONG ENOUGH TO GET THE LESSON AND THEN KEEP THAT SHIT MOVING. YOU'VE GOT TO LOOK TOWARDS THE FUTURE BECAUSE WHAT'S IN THE PAST CAN'T BE ALTERED. THINK ABOUT AND WORK TOWARD THINGS THAT CAN BE DONE RIGHT NOW, NOT WHAT ALREADY WAS. THEN GET BUSY TO MAKE THAT SHIT HAPPEN.

Photo by Thomas Jacobi

TRACK 45

DATE September 10, 2013
ARTIST 2 Chainz
ALBUMS *B.O.A.T.S. II*
PRODUCED "U Da Realest"

> *"IF YOU DON'T HAVE TIME TO DO IT RIGHT, THEN YOU DON'T HAVE TIME TO DO IT AT ALL."*
> —DRUMMA BOY

2 Chainz held the king of trap title during this era. He was the hottest rapper out coming off his Gold and Grammy-nominated debut album, *Based on a T.R.U. Story*, and he had absolutely no intentions of slowing down. He stuck to the script by staying in the creative zone, and he capitalized off this momentum by giving the people what they wanted, which was more trapped out music.

I produced "U Da Realest," where 2 Chainz flows from that emotional center that conveys the story he wanted to tell— a hood tribute to fallen street soldiers. This is one of my favorite beats I've done for him, and you can hear in his voice the passion and feel the homage he's paying to those he's lost. It trips me out to know how universal music is, giving people a view of human's relationships. 2 Chainz delivered a clever approach with his wordplay and wanted his message to be heard and felt.

There are certain beats that only certain artists can do justice to. Soon as I hit play for 2 Chainz, he walked into the booth and spazzed out. It was like an instant light bulb that came on… "I can't explain it how I'm getting to the payments, rest in peace to my nigga god bless all his babies." He had his homegirl record some background vocals on the hook and throughout the song. In less than an hour, we had a prolific anthem.

This album might be my favorite 2 Chainz album too. It's just real and honest and matter of fact. It was also a seasoned group of production talent and guest features, but none of that celebrity light outshined my boy's lyrical prowess. That's just pure genius talent. I was also in the studio when Pharrell made "Feds Watching." He came in the studio with a tuxedo on and a laptop computer and cooked up the beat in about 30 minutes. I was like, "Damn, this guy doing just how we do it and overall energy was so polite and classy." I already had so much respect for Pharrell but that definitely gave a stamp of approval and motivation for "U Da Realest," which we recorded right after.

---

2 Chainz released his second studio album *B.O.A.T.S. II: Me Time* on September 10, 2013, by Def Jam Recordings. The album peaked at #3 on the *Billboard* 200 and #2 on the Top R&B/Hip-Hop Albums. It sold 63,000 copies in its first week.

D-BOY TALK

I DON'T BELIEVE THAT GOD CREATED ANY OF US BY MISTAKE. WE ALL HAVE A SPECIFIC PURPOSE TO PURSUE AND CARRY OUT WHILE WE STILL HAVE AIR PUMPING THROUGH OUR LUNGS.

I TRULY BELIEVE THAT EVERYONE, WHETHER READING OR LISTENING TO THE AUDIO VERSION OF THIS BOOK, HAS SOMETHING TO CONTRIBUTE TO THIS EARTH REGARDLESS OF WHAT HIS CIRCUMSTANCES MAY LOOK LIKE OR WHAT HE'S BEEN THROUGH.

TRACK 45: 2 CHAINZ

FROM NOW ON, LOOK AT YOURSELF AS A KING OR QUEEN AND UNDERSTAND THAT SUCCESS IS YOUR BIRTHRIGHT. BE ALL THAT GOD INTENDED YOU TO BE SO THAT WHEN YOU LEAVE THIS EARTH, YOU WILL HAVE GIVEN THIS LIFE EVERYTHING YOU HAD TO GIVE.

IN SPORTS, THEY SAY, "LEAVE IT ALL ON THE FIELD." IN OTHER WORDS, WHENEVER YOU HAVE AN OPPORTUNITY TO PLAY THE GAME, GIVE IT ALL YOU'VE GOT EACH AND EVERY TIME. DON'T PLAY IT SAFE BUT PUT IT ALL ON THE LINE. WHEN YOU APPROACH LIFE LIKE THIS, YOU WILL HAVE LITTLE IF ANY REGRETS BECAUSE YOU DIDN'T HOLD BACK. LIVE YOUR LIFE AND LIVE YOUR DREAM.

Photo by Thomas Jacobi

TRACK 46

DATE March 11, 2014
ARTIST Ledisi
ALBUMS *The Truth*
PRODUCED "Rock With You" featuring Jerry Wonda (written by Johntá Austin)

"TRUTH IS ALWAYS YOUR BEST DEFENSE."
-DRUMMA BOY

I have been blessed to collaborate with the best of the best in the business, including soul singer, Ledisi. She's a real artist's artist, and that is what I loved about working with her; I knew it would be special. She sang with the New Orleans Symphony Orchestra as a kid. With my dad being a historical part of the Memphis Symphony Orchestra and raising me to know every note on the musical scale and play multiple instruments, I think he thought I would be more of this kind of producer. But either way, I was grateful to have the opportunity to put this credit on my discography.

I know I've mentioned this before, but I thrive off having a diverse catalog. I don't like being pigeonholed or feel like my talent has a cap on it. I wasn't raised to think like that. I can produce hits across multiple categories.

The Truth was Ledisi's seventh album, and I had the honor of producing "Rock With You" with Jerry Wonda and written by my homeboy, Johntá Austin. I met Jerry Wonda in New York using his studio Platinum Sound, working with another label, and Johntá was family by the way of Noontime. My manager is Johntá's manager as well, so it's one big team. Relationships have always been a key part of my career and landing placements.

Jerry "Wonda" Duplessis' first major success as a producer was for the Fugees' 1996 album *The Score*. He also played the bass guitar with the Fugees, and group member, Wyclef Jean, is his cousin. Johntá Austin is an American singer-songwriter, arranger, producer, vocalist, and rapper. Signed to Jermaine Dupri's So So Def Recordings, Austin was awarded two Grammy Awards for his work on the songs "We Belong Together" by Mariah Carey and "Be Without You" by Mary J. Blige.

I had fun rhythmically adding hi-hats and claps and exercising a different part of my brain. The up-tempo beat was a departure from Ledisi's previous recordings that centered on the heavy soul, jazz, and R&B. You can hear her letting go and having fun on this track, which was cool to contribute to because it meant I took part in navigating through unchartered territory with her.

These are the type of alignments that push the envelope on artistic excellence. Taking a well-documented trap and Hip-Hop producer and successfully pairing him with a demonstrated vocal powerhouse is epic shit. I thrive on going against the grain. I like veering into unchartered territory; it strengthens my confidence in knowing that I have the capability to do groundbreaking and legendary shit.

> **Ledisi's *The Truth*, released on March 11, 2014, peaked at #14 on the US *Billboard* 200 and #6 on the Top R&B/Hip-Hop Albums.**

TRACK 46: LEDISI

D-BOY TALK

My first check from a label came from J. Prince himself. He taught me the difference between cash money and having bank accounts. My big bruh, Ensayne Wayne, plugged me in with Double Dose Records, and it was no turning back.

Dedicated hustle, a strong work ethic, and premeditated decisions landed me a great relationship. In 2002, I had three records on Tela's album at $2,500 per track during my second year in college at the University of Memphis. That bread helped me beat my dad's #100KINTHEBANKCHALLENGE.

TRACK 47

DATE April 15th, 2014
ARTIST August Alsina
ALBUMS *The Testimony*
PRODUCED "No Love," "FML," and "No Love" featuring Nicki Minaj (remix)

"LOYALTY AND RESPECT ARE EARNED, NEVER BOUGHT."
-DRUMMA BOY

After working with Ledisi, I was excited when I got the call from my manager, Squeak, saying he had just gotten off the phone with Henry "Noonie" Lee, owner of Noontime. He said he had a new artist named August Alsina that he wanted me to work with. I knew this was another major opportunity to show my musicianship with another R&B recording artist.

The first session we did together was at 11th Street Studios. At the time, he had his first single out "I Luv This Shit." I made sure I had my cameraman, Ben Styles, there to capture the moment visually. There were two studio rooms locked down for us, the A-room and the B-room. For two days, we recorded as many songs as possible and vibed out. Out of that lockout, I ended up with two songs on the album.

Testimony was August Alsina's debut album that hit #2 on the *Billboard* 200 chart. His music cinematically told these hood stories that could rival any street rapper. However, his narrative wasn't a reflection of his skills as a singer. August represented a new era of R&B.

I did two records on his culturally relevant project, and one was released as the second single, "No Love," a remix featuring Nicki Minaj. I treated that particular beat like a Hip-Hop track and just added a melody along with a smooth bass line to complement his vocals. As a new artist, he knew exactly what type of sound he wanted and was very interactive with the writing process.

August is a real student of music; collaborating in the studio with him was a pleasure because he made suggestions that stemmed from an educated standpoint. You gotta respect those people who are not only talented but who also respect their gift enough to improve upon it, which includes doing the homework. He knew as much about me as I knew about him, and I think that just reflects the kind of passion and love he has for music.

August Alsina released *Testimony* on April 15, 2014, by Def Jam Recordings. It was supported by six singles including "I Luv This Shit," "Ghetto," "Numb," "Make It Home," "Kissin' on My Tattoos," and "No Love." The album reached #2 on the US *Billboard* 200 and #1 on the Top R&B/Hip-Hop Albums. *Testimony* was certified RIAA Gold in March of 2006 and RIAA Platinum on September 1, 2021. "No Love" was certified RIAA Platinum on October 13, 2015 and was later certified 2x platinum by the RIAA on April 21, 2021.

TRACK 47: AUGUST ALSINA

D-BOY TALK

WHILE YOU'RE OUT HERE GETTING IT OUT OF THE MUD, USE SOME OF YOUR DOWNTIME TO PREPARE FOR THE SUCCESS YOU ARE ASKING FOR BECAUSE ONCE YOU GET ON, YOU'VE GOT TO BE ABLE TO MOVE QUICKLY. MAKE SURE YOU'RE STUDYING THE FOUNDERS OF THE BUSINESS AS WELL AS THE NEW FOLKS OUT HERE MAKING MOVES. THERE'S NOTHING LIKE KNOWING THE HISTORY OF THE BUSINESS YOU'RE IN AND HAVING THAT RESPECT FOR THE CRAFT. DEVELOP A CONSISTENT WORK ETHIC NOW SO THAT YOU'LL ALREADY BE CONDITIONED FOR THE MARATHON WHEN YOU START MOVING.

Photo by Dominic Fondon

TRACK 48

DATE September 2, 2014
ARTIST Young Jeezy
ALBUMS Seen It All: The Autobiography
PRODUCED "Me Ok"

> "WHEN YOU ARE WHO YOU SAY YOU ARE, THAT'S LIKE HAVING SUPERNATURAL POWERS."
> -DRUMMA BOY

Five months had gone by since working with August when I was back at it with Jeezy for *Seen It All: The Autobiography*. By this time, everyone knew what to expect because of our chemistry and the history of hits. It's crazy how I went from doing an intro song, "Standing Ovation" on *TM101*, to a lead single "Put On," to another lead single "Lose My Mind," to my third lead single with Jeezy "Me Ok," on the Snowman's fifth album.

Jeezy kept his word on staying down with me after I pulled through for him on his debut album. You must establish yourself in the game without waiting on validation, permission, or a stamp from anybody. Nobody is entitled to help you nor show their loyalty to you. Those are earned, and I knew he had a forever respect for me.

I was blessed to have solid people around me who also believed in me and valued my skill level, but that's not always the case. Take control of your career by deciding to do work you believe in versus working hard and letting people tell you what you're going to do. There's a difference.

I like how Jeezy carved his own lane when he came in the game and stayed there. He has never tried to be anything more or less than what his music talks about; it's why he's now considered a legacy artist. I wanted to keep the song rooted in who Jeezy is as a trap star, which is raw, lyrical, pensive, and creative.

Anytime Jeezy is ready to get back in the studio, he will call like, "Yoooo I need that plate mane where it's at?"

I would always have a pack ready to send or pull up on him with, but this time I wanted to present something new and fresh. I started this beat off with the pianos and then the 808 to make sure it had a certain bounce to it. Wishing in thirty minutes, I was done with the beat then sent it to Jeezy via email. He sent me flame emojis back, and the rest was history.

We're inevitably going to get a final installment in the TM series. When it's all said and done, Jeezy's complete body of work will go down as one of the best in the game. I'm blessed to not only have touched almost every album since he officially debuted, but to also have received Grammy nominations as well as platinum and gold plaques from a relationship that started when I was a kid.

The seventh studio album by Jeezy, *Seen It All: The Autobiography*, was released on September 2, 2014, and debuted at #2 on the US *Billboard* 200, selling 121,000 copies in its first week. The album peaked at #1 on Top R&B/Hip-Hop Albums and reached #8 on the Canadian Albums. *Seen It All* is certified gold by the RIAA.

TRACK 48: YOUNG JEEZY
D-BOY TALK

THE FIRST BEATS I MADE WERE ON CASSETTE TAPES. THAT'S HOW FAR MY HISTORY GOES BACK IN THIS GAME. I DIDN'T TAKE SHORTCUTS, AND I URGE YOU NOT TO EITHER. WHEN YOU DO, YOU CUT YOURSELF SHORT OF THE OPPORTUNITY TO EDUCATE YOURSELF ON WHAT IT ACTUALLY TAKES TO CREATE A SOLID FOUNDATION. THE KIND OF CONFIDENCE YOU GET WHEN YOU GET IT OFF THE CURB IS UNPARALLELED, AND NOBODY CAN TAKE THAT FROM YOU. DON'T CHEAT YOURSELF; TREAT YOURSELF TO THE DISCIPLINE OF HARD WORK.

TRACK 49

DATE July 16, 2015
ARTIST Gucci Mane
ALBUMS Wilt Chamberlain Part 5
PRODUCED "I Think I Love Her" featuring Ester Dean

"REPEAT BUSINESS IS THE BEST COMPLIMENT YOU CAN GET."
— DRUMMA BOY

People have always asked me how I'm able to work with Young Jeezy and Gucci Mane or if either of the two have an issue with me working with the other. I just focus on making good music and feeding it to the people. As a producer, we make the music, but it's hard to control what artists say or how they express themselves on a record.

It's funny because I remember Gucci coming up to me in the studio one time laughing like, "Aye Drum, I ain't gone lie you got Jeezy on fire I need something like that." I laughed back like, "Mane, you crazy; I got something different for you, fasho!" Gucci was the one always cracking jokes, and having fun, and his personality made you wanna work with him.

Everybody is a fan of Gucci and tapped into his music heavily. Gucci and I dropped so many projects and songs people knew our relationship was close. Polow da Don hit me up one day saying to pull up; he had some studio time at Zak's Recording Studio and wanted Gucci to fall through. I was like, that's an easy no brainer call for the win column.

I reached out to Gucci and told him Polow wanted us to pull up. We arranged the times and made it happen! I made the "I Think I Luv Her" beat in about ten minutes and ended up collaborating on production with Polow on the second beat I made for Lloyd called "Twerk Off," featuring Juicy J. Gucci shouted out me and Polow on the song "I Think I Luv Her" so many people think he may have produced this one, but Gucci was showing love since it was his session and he got Ester Dean on the song.

D-BOY TALK

DON'T BE TIMID ABOUT ASKING FOR WHAT YOU WANT IN THIS BUSINESS OR IN LIFE, PERIOD. THE WORST THAT COULD HAPPEN IS THEY SAY "NO," BUT YOU HAVEN'T LOST ANYTHING. YOU'RE NO BETTER OR NO WORSE; HOWEVER, AT LEAST YOU HAVE PEACE OF MIND INSTEAD OF WONDERING WHAT COULD'VE BEEN. IF THE OUTCOME IS IN THE AFFIRMATIVE, YOU GAINED WHAT YOU WANTED, AND YOU DEVELOPED THAT MUSCLE OF SPEAKING UP. ALWAYS BE ASSERTIVE ABOUT WHAT YOU WANT YET RESPECTFUL. IT'S A WAY TO GET YOUR POINT ACROSS WITHOUT COMING ACROSS LIKE AN ASSHOLE.

Photo by Dominic Fondon

Photo by Mike Asgaurdian

TRACK 50

DATE October 30, 2015
ARTIST Migos
MIXTAPE *Back to the Bando*
PRODUCED The Single "Look at my Dab"

> *"YOU EVER NOTICE THAT IN EVERY CLASS OF SOCIETY, GRATITUDE IS THE RAREST OF ALL HUMAN VIRTUES."*
> —DRUMMA BOY

Every time I have a beat on a new project, I get calls from more artists wanting to work and get in the studio. "I Think I Luv Her" was going crazy in the clubs, and everyone was reaching out. I remember getting a DM on Twitter from the Migos account with an email in the message. I saw that the Twitter page was verified, so I took a chance and emailed five beats. If you can't get it in five beats, you ain't gone get it.

This was one of those records that you just know in your bones it's going to do something. After I did the track and then heard the Migos flow over it, I knew it was out of here; the energy was just too crazy. This song was leaked on the mixtape *Back to the Bando*. It took off organically throughout the clubs and sports scene. Seeing everybody from grandparents to kids doing the dab was definitely pretty cool. It always feels good seeing the world have so much fun to your music.

"Look at my Dab" had a crazy buzz behind it because the dance move known as the "dab" amplified its popularity; everybody was into the song and dance. Despite how it may seem like the Migos just took off out of nowhere, those boys earned the success they are enjoying now.

When I first started working with them, they reminded me a lot of a young Gucci. They were very driven, focused, and had distinct personalities. I take pride in creating records that turn into movements like "Look at My Dab."

This mixtape song was bigger than what the chart numbers reflected because its cultural relevance and impact can't be quantified. While it only peaked at #87 on *Billboard*'s Hot 100 chart, you couldn't go anywhere during this time and not hear this record along with seeing people doing the dab dance. From figures in sports (Cam Newton) and politics (Hilary Clinton) to members of the Royal Family in Oslo (Prince Sverre Magnus of Norway) and international Presidents (Uhuru Kenyatta of Kenya, Emmanuel Macron of France), the dab dance inspired by the song was a global phenomenon.

> "Look at My Dab" was released on October 30, 2015 as a single by Migos on Quality Control Music and 300 Entertainment. It peaked at #87 on the US *Billboard* Hot 100, #28 on the Hot R&B/Hip-Hop Songs and #16 Hot Rap Songs.

D-BOY TALK

DON'T EVER CHASE THE MONEY. INSTEAD, LET IT CHASE YOU.

AND YOU LET IT CHASE YOU BY STAYING TRUE TO YOUR VISION, YOUR PURPOSE, AND REMEMBERING WHY YOU STARTED IN THE BEGINNING.

WHEN I FIRST STARTED, MY PURPOSE WAS TO HONOR WHAT I WAS PASSIONATE ABOUT. I FELT LIKE I OWED THAT TO MYSELF

TRACK 49: MIGOS

TO UNCOVER WHY I COULDN'T SHAKE MY DESIRE TO WANT TO BE IN THE STUDIO AND MAKE MUSIC.

SO, I DID IT.

THE MONEY CAME TO ME AS A BYPRODUCT OF MY PASSION.

I WAS NEVER PRESSED ABOUT BREAD, EVEN ON MY BROKEST OF DAYS BECAUSE THAT'S NOT WHAT MOTIVATED ME. MAKING A DOPER BEAT THAN WHAT I HAD MADE THE DAY BEFORE WAS WHAT DROVE ME. LEARNING MORE ABOUT MY CRAFT FUELED ME. MAKING PROGRESSION, EVEN IF IT WAS ONLY MAKING ENOUGH MONEY TO EAT AND PUT GAS IN THE CAR, I WAS GOOD WITH THAT. AS A RESULT OF MY BEING SERIOUS AND FOCUSED ABOUT BEING A PRODUCER, IN ADDITION TO HUSTLING EVERYWHERE, I THOUGHT I COULD MEET SOMEBODY THAT NEEDED BEATS— THE MONEY CAME.

IT ALWAYS COMES WHEN YOU PUT THE PASSION FIRST.

Photo by Thomas Jacobi

TRACK 51

DATE February 19, 2016
ARTIST Young Dolph
ALBUM *King of Memphis*
PRODUCED "Both Ways"

"ONE THING ABOUT ME, IF I FUCK WITH YOU, WE LOCKED IN FOR LIFE REGARDLESS OF WHAT YOU GOING THRU."
-DRUMMA BOY

Working with the emerging hometown heat is like having a badge of honor to me. Memphis is where it all began, and it's the city that birthed and raised me into the man I am. When I first started, I was thankful to have my brother, who was plugging me with artists he knew and making plays for me. I always wanted to be that plug in return to my city. At this time, I had records on Dolph's album and Gotti's album. People would always ask how I managed working with both of them and I always said I mind my business and just focus on the business. Both of them handling they business with me and that's all that mattered.

One thing about Dolph, he always had his own hustle and never really had to rely on music. Those types of artists are always the easiest to work with because the business gets handled. Dolph, Rocko, Gucci, Gotti, Jeezy, Plies, and T.I. all understood the hustle as well as the business and look at where they are in their careers now. Even guys like Money Bagg Yo, Blacc Youngsta, Pooh Shiesty, and Lil Migo all understand that hustle and allows them to fund themselves.

Consistency is so essential in this music business. People get put on to new artists so quickly. If you take too long to drop new music, people will forget about you. Dolph reminded me of Gucci Mane how fast he was able to get you another project back-to-back. People would always make jokes that Gucci Mane's work ethic was like 2Pac, and Dolph had that ethic.

I knew that Young Dolph's, *King of Memphis*, would bring a lot of attention due to the controversy. You've got to be willing to put it all on the line if that's how you really feel. On a marketing tip, the title alone made people want to hear the album full of production from me— TM88, Mike Will, Zaytoven, Nard & B, and more. Regardless of what people thought, it had folks thinking and talking.

People consider me to be overconfident, but I'd rather put myself in the category of where I want to be than where I'm at. I'd rather aim too high and miss the mark than aim too low and hit that shit.

I did the record "Both Ways," and as soon as the listener pressed play, I wanted to set the tone with hard-hitting drums. Like Gucci, Dolph wanted his beats ready and didn't want to waste time in the studio making beats, so I always had a folder ready. He never disappointed with the bossed-up lyrics that sound like a man that's lived twice his age. I've always been a fan of rappers who have a genuine story to tell, and they're able to tell it in a compelling way that almost anybody from any walk of life and generation can understand. Dolph was like that. Obviously, he had a lot to prove before crowning himself the King of Memphis, but then again, as I wrote previously, you've got to see yourself bigger than what you may be in order to actually get there. I salute the young homie.

Young Dolph's debut album *King of Memphis* was released on February 19, 2016, by Paper Route Empire (P.R.E). Additional production included Mike Will Made It, TM88, Zaytoven, Nard & B, and more. *King Of Memphis* reached #9 on US *Billboard* Top R&B/Hip-Hop Albums, #49 on the *Billboard* 200 and #5 Top Rap Albums and Independent Albums.

TRACK 51: YOUNG DOLPH

D-BOY TALK

THERE ARE CERTAIN THINGS THAT COME WITH TALENT; TALENT IS 10% OF THE INDUSTRY, BUT THE OTHER 90% IS BUSINESS. A LOT OF PEOPLE TALK ABOUT BREAKING THE RULES, BUT BEFORE YOU CAN BREAK THEM, YOU'VE GOT TO UNDERSTAND WHAT THEY ARE. THAT'S THE BUSINESS PART. YOU CAN'T DISRUPT WHAT YOU DON'T UNDERSTAND.

TRACK 52

DATE February 19, 2016
ARTIST Yo Gotti
ALBUM *The Art of Hustle*
PRODUCED "Imagine That"

> "YOU CAN'T DO GENIUS SHIT WITH GENERIC PEOPLE."
> —DRUMMA BOY

I think the fact that I have dozens of production credits with Gotti exemplifies the importance of how maintaining a good relationship with people can serve you far beyond doing just one or two records. We always respected each other and proud of each other's success. Whenever we link up, you know it's going to be epic.

In this album, Gotti was emphasizing loyalty and going back to fuck with everybody he started out with. Gotti reached out for a pack and was like, "I need ya on this album." When I get called, I got to go into hibernation and seclude myself from everyone. I'll lock myself in the house and just cook up for a few days. Out of fifteen beats I made in those two days, I mixed down my favorite five and sent them to Gotti.

I didn't hear the song until the album was released, and I enjoy that process sometimes because it gives me something to look forward to as a fan. Sometimes when you get copies of the music, you've played it so much that when it comes out, it's old to you.

The Art of the Hustle debuted at #4 on the *Billboard* 200 chart, and I produced the record "Imagine That." I'd go so far as to say this was the album that propelled

Gotti into that main-mainstream's spotlight. It goes to show that you can be in this business for years, even decades before you get recognized on a global scale. I think that's why I like working with Gotti; he's a real hustler— hence the project's name. He has always had a passion for rap, and his dedication to the art and craft of Hip-Hop is what makes him one of the best to ever do it.

> On February 19, 2016, Yo Gotti released his 8th album, *The Art of Hustle*. The album debuted at #4 on the US *Billboard* 200 chart, selling 61,000 copies in its first week. *The Art of Hustle* topped the Top R&B/Hip-Hop Albums chart at #1 and sold over 500,000 copies making it RIAA Gold certified.

D-BOY TALK

ONE THING I CAN SAY ABOUT ME IS THAT I DON'T REST ON MY BUTT OR USE ANY "BUTS." YOU KNOW THOSE PEOPLE WHO SAY STUFF LIKE, "I WAS GOING TO START TODAY, BUT...," "I WANT TO SUPPORT, BUT...," OR "I WANT TO GO, BUT...." ALL THOSE "BUTS" ARE EXCUSES. WE ALL HAVE THINGS TO DO, PLACES TO BE, AND PEOPLE TO SEE, BUT WE MAKE TIME AND ARRANGEMENTS FOR WHAT WE DEEM AS IMPORTANT. SOME FOLKS WILL BLAME EVERYBODY BUT THEMSELVES AS TO WHY THEY CONTINUE TO REMAIN STUCK IN THE SAME CIRCUMSTANCES WHEN THEY NEED TO LOOK IN THE MIRROR TO DISCOVER THE REAL PROBLEM. GET OFF YA BUTS, MANE.

Photo by Robert Ector

TRACK 53

DATE July 22, 2016
ARTIST Gucci Mane
ALBUM *Everybody Looking*
PRODUCED "All My Children"

"IF YOU LOVE LIFE, IT WILL LOVE YOU BACK TENFOLD."
-DRUMMA BOY

This was another time Gucci Mane had gotten out of jail. This time felt different though like he was out for good. He would normally book a studio and be right back to recording. Instead, he was with his wife and spending lots of time organizing his life. Maybe about a month after he was out, I got a text from his lawyer saying Gucci wanted me to pull up to his house. They had to do a background check on me, and once I was approved, I went out to his house.

When I arrived, he met me outside and showed me around his new house. We caught up for hours, reminiscing off old times about random sessions in different cities. It was crazy to me he always knew my number by heart. You heard so many stories that Gucci was a clone and this and that. I knew all that was bullshit. Just talking to him like it's no one you remembering all this if you're a clone, thinking to myself.

We went into his studio room, and he had all these notes on the wall from jail of songs that he had written. It almost felt like a part of the trap museum how it was all arranged neatly, title by title. I plugged up my USB drive and started playing beats, setting a vibe to see which idea he wanted to do first. I got to the third beat, and he yelled out, "That's it, Drum, pull it up."

In traditional Gucci fashion, the record was put together relatively quickly. He only had three guests appearances on the entire project: Kanye, Drake, and Young Thug. The record ended being titled "All My Children," and this was another easy alley-oop from Kobe to Shaq. Having beats ready for Gucci is always easy— make the beat bounce, keep it hood, over simple drums. I knew people wanted to hear him rhyme and not just vibe out to the beat, and I think he provided both.

> **Gucci's first album in five years and ninth overall studio album, *Everybody Looking*, dropped on July 22, 2016. It hit #2 on the US *Billboard* 200 and #1 on the Top R&B/Hip-Hop Albums, selling 68,000 units. The album was certified RIAA Gold, selling over 500,000 copies on June 30, 2022.**

TRACK 53: GUCCI MANE

D-BOY TALK

Understand the process and commitment it's going to take before you start investing your time and money into something blindly because you saw it work for somebody else. What works for them may not work for you. I know folks who dumped their savings into building out studios and assumed that when they turned on their "open for business" signs, people would flock in, and they'd start recouping their money ASAP. But when it doesn't happen that way or that quickly, they get impatient and frustrated and want to quit. They didn't do enough homework and research or have the passion to continue going when the business didn't pop off how they wanted.

TRACK 54

DATE September 20, 2016
ARTIST Gucci Mane
ALBUM Woptober
PRODUCED "Out The Zoo"

> "THERE IS PAIN IN THE PROCESS, BUT THERE'S ALSO PURPOSE THERE TOO THAT LEADS TO PROFIT."
> —DRUMMA BOY

Usually, every time Gucci drops a project, I'm on it. There will be some albums or projects here and there that I might miss, but we are always locked in most of the time. We have over one hundred songs together, so it's like playing basketball for real and just doing what you do best. This project came about pretty quickly because that's just how he works, always wanting to keep music circulating in the streets. His work ethic is unmatched and reminds me of how I move, so I can relate.

When Gucci reached out, he said he was in the studio, but I was in another city, so I emailed a pack over to him so he could work. A couple of weeks later, I got a call back from Gucci telling me which beat he used and got the files ready for the mix. We move quickly and efficiently even from long distances.

On the mixtape *Woptober*, I did the track "Out The Zoo," which is a mid-tempo beat but has a slower pace. I wanted Gucci to flow without having to compete with the distractions of too much bass or instrumentation. It's stripped down so fans can hear Gucci do what Gucci does best, which is kick real shit in a stylized and charismatic way.

Gucci Mane released his mixtape *Woptober* on October 14, 2016. The mixtape peaked at #43 on the *Billboard* 200. Released on Atlantic Records and GUWOP Enterprises the mixtape features appearances from Rick Ross and Young Dolph.

D-BOY TALK

GET YOUR BUSINESS AFFAIRS IN ORDER. THE NUMBER ONE THING I DO IS START THE PROCESS OF HAVING MY BEAT COPYRIGHTED AS SOON AS I MAKE IT. I SEND IT OFF THE NEXT DAY. JUST IN CASE AN ARTIST THINKS HE CAN CHUCK THE DEUCES ON ME, I'M GOOD. I'M NOT ABOUT TALKING IT OUT IN THE STREETS; WE CAN DO THAT IN COURT. I KEEP IT REAL, SIMPLE, PLAIN, AND STRAIGHT UP. THE SECOND THING I SUGGEST IS TO GET A REPUTABLE LAWYER BECAUSE WITHOUT THE CONTRACTS, YOU AIN'T TALKING ABOUT SHIT. WITHOUT SIGNING A W-9, YOU'RE NOT GETTING A CHECK; WITHOUT SIGNING A PRODUCER AGREEMENT, YOU'RE NOT GETTING PAID. EVEN IF YOU DECIDE TO WORK UNDER THE TABLE, YOU NEED SOME TYPE OF AGREEMENT IN PLACE. YOU NEVER KNOW THAT RECORD COULD BLOW UP, AND YOU'LL NEVER GET PAID NOR THE CREDIT.

Photo by: Robert Lector

Photo by Thomas Jacobi

TRACK 55

DATE April 1, 2017
ARTIST Young Dolph
ALBUM *Bulletproof*
PRODUCED "How I Feel" featuring Gucci Mane

"YOU'RE ONLY GOING TO GO AS FAR AS YOUR MIND GROWS."
-DRUMMA BOY

Working with Dolph was a special collab because it was somewhat of a full-circle moment for me. He was a Memphis native who was pushing the city's culture forward, and I like having a direct influence on this new generation of artists.

Since I started in the business as a teenager, I'm like a young OG with two solid decades in the game, so to connect with young guys like him is a rewarding feeling.

I produced the record "How I Feel" that featured Gucci Mane from Dolph's sophomore album *Bulletproof*. The energy Dolph brought to the record reminded me of a twenty-something Gucci, where it was just raw and uncensored; every word he spit had real emotion behind it. When you have that kind of chemistry going in the studio, you know you've got something special, and the people get to experience the vibe through the music.

As a producer, you see so much going up with these artists, and it's almost a cheat code of what type of music to present. Many of these guys have amazing stories to tell and need the best fit for them to feel comfortable enough to say what's on their minds. Different beats will bring out certain things as you try to deliver what's in your head.

I honestly was surprised Dolph picked that beat, but when I heard the finished song featuring Gucci, I saw his vision and where he was going with it. It's crazy how so many times we make beats for a particular artist, and it will end up with a completely different artist. When you're a work wire, you don't always do what makes you happy, you do what makes your client happy.

Young Dolph released his second album, Bulletproof on April 1, 2017, on Paper Route Empire. The album reached #36 on the US Billboard 200, #19 on Top R&B/Hip-Hop Albums, #14 on Top Rap Albums and #7 Independent Albums.

TRACK 55: YOUNG DOLPH

D-BOY TALK

I DON'T SUBSCRIBE TO THAT "FAKE IT TILL YOU MAKE IT" MINDSET, BUT I BELIEVE THAT YOU SHOULD ACT LIKE WHO AND WHAT YOU WANT TO BECOME. I HAD A SET SCHEDULE EVERY DAY ON WHEN I'D MAKE BEATS, JUST LIKE I HAD READ HOW THE SUCCESSFUL PRODUCERS DID. WHEN I WAS IN THE STUDIO WITH MY BROTHER AS A KID, I'D JUST OBSERVE. I WANTED TO LISTEN TO WHAT WAS BEING SAID AND HOW THEY SAID IT. I WATCHED WHAT THEY DID BEHIND THE BOARDS. I WATCHED HOW THEY INTERACTED WITH THE ENGINEER, THE ARTIST, AND THE STUDIO MANAGER. SO, WHEN I HAD MY FIRST SESSION, I MIRRORED THE SAME THINGS I HAD SEEN AND HEARD BUT WITH MY PERSONALITY.

TRACK 56

DATE October 17, 2017
ARTIST Young Dolph
ALBUM *Thinking Out Loud*
PRODUCED "While U Here"

"TRY TO SELF-EDUCATE INSTEAD OF SELF-MEDICATE."
— DRUMMA BOY

This was a crazy time for Dolph. He had dodged death a couple of times that year and had been in stable condition after being shot multiple times. Thankfully, he pulled through and recovered. Clearly, we gave him space, but as soon as he called and said, "Send me something," please believe the pack was sent.

This record was heavy and poignant because you could tell he was delivering every word from the heart about his experience and appreciating your loved ones while you still have air pumping through your lungs. You could tell after experiencing something like that, he was appreciating life differently. I was happy he was ok and here to see his kids grow up and continue releasing music.

I wanted the beat to be simple and not to overshadow his lyrics' sincerity. Yet, I also added in some 808 to highlight the severity of Dolph's situation. I wanted the song to sound like a movie when it first hit, so that's why you hear a lot of drama with the horns and the strings. Three of the album's songs were released as promotional singles. "While U Here" was released as the album's first single on October 16, 2017. While "Believe Me" and "Drippy" were released as the second and third singles.

The third album by Young Dolph, *Thinking Out Loud*, was dropped on October 20, 2017. It debuted at #16 on the US *Billboard* 200, #9 on the Top R&B/Hip-Hop Albums, #8 on Top Rap Albums and #2 Independent Album charts.

D-BOY TALK

Get outside of your comfort zone and take risks. I've accomplished every big goal because I did something before I was ready, and I bet on myself. A long life ain't promised, so do what you can while you can. People only see a fraction of how busy I am on social media, and I have loved ones who'll reach out telling me to slow down. But I got dreams to fulfill, and I make sure when my head hits the pillow every night that I made the most out of the 24-hours God blessed me with. I'd rather suffer in the short-term than live life with long-term regret.

Photo by Thomas Jacobi

TRACK 57

DATE April 27, 2018
ARTIST YoungBoy Never Broke Again
ALBUM *Until Death Call My Name*
PRODUCED "We Poppin'" featuring Birdman

> "NEVER LOOK AT YOUR SCARS AS BEING UGLY.
> IT JUST MEANS THAT YOU'RE STRONGER
> THAN WHATEVER TRIED TO HURT YOU."
> — DRUMMA BOY

I made this beat at the House of Hits studio that I helped build and brand in Atlanta. Young Greatness (RIP) was alive at the time and he set up a session at my studio and said he was going to have Birdman pull up. So, it originally started as a Young Greatness and Birdman's session but when Birdman got there, he pulled me and Greatness to the side and said he wanted to have NBA come through. He knew it was our session but out of respect asked if we'd be cool if we let NBA Youngboy knock out a song.

I remember saying something like, "Hell nah I don't mind, especially if I do the beat." I knew this young dude had a crazy buzz and could rap like crazy. I had always been a fan of the OG Birdman as well, so we all agreed on making some magic happen. I played about five beats and he was like, "Pull that up." He asked if we could clear the room out for a minute and let him just vibe, me and him. He said this first verse "Imma write for Birdman and have him re-rap it and the second verse gone be mine." I was like, "Ok bet lets knock it out." I would say he knocked out the song in about 45 minutes then Birdman came in and did the first verse over. In less than 2 hours, we had another hit on our hands. A few weeks later, the video was shot and released!

I cooked this beat up using the MPC X and Akai software as things are more digital than analog these days. Still the sound of the digital wave is fresh, clear, and warm! It's all about your ear overall and being able to mix the best sounds together for any artist to tell their story. I wanted to ease up from the traditional gangster sound and deliver an easier on the ear sound with the chords being uplifting and making you want to think positively and embark on the dues we've paid. Now we are celebrating the hard work we put in and that's how this song makes me feel.

I cooked this beat up using the MPC X and Akai software as things are more digital than analog these days. Still the sound of the digital wave is fresh, clear and warm! Its all about your ear overall and being able to mix the best sounds together for any artist to tell their story. I wanted ease up from the traditional gangster sound and deliver an easier on the ear sound with the chords being uplifting and making you want to think positively and embark on the dues we've paid. Now we are celebrating the hard work we put in and that's how this song makes me feel.

I ended with this song because ironically I lost my brother in Feb 2018 and death called my name. I took the rest of this year working diligently to complete the formation of his estate and to ensure his four children: Raven, Devon, Jordan, and Selena Miles were all assisted with guidance and support. This book is dedicated to my blood brother, Ferrell Wayne Miles, aka Ensayne Wayne.

> **YoungBoy Never Broke Again** released his debut album *Until Death Call My Name* on April 27, 2018, under Never Broke Again and Atlantic Records. The album debuted at #7 on the US *Billboard* 200 with 43,000 copies in its first week. It peaked at #5 Top R&B/Hip-Hop Albums and #4 Top Rap Albums and broke into the Canadian Albums charts reaching #38. It was certified RIAA Gold in July 2018, platinum in January of 2019 and 2x RIAA Platinum on May 30, 2023.

TRACK 57: YOUNGBOY NEVER BROKE AGAIN

D-BOY TALK

I wake up and answer to God and my life before picking up a phone. Take time in the morning to get your thoughts and plans together and then attack the day. People will blow you up about a favor and then can't even pay for it when it's on the table. Stay focused and use your time wisely.

Photo by Dominic Fondon

NO LIFE WITHOUT MUSIC

Creating music has been my greatest joy in life; I couldn't imagine a world without it. Having the ear to recognize distinct sounds, the foresight to make pivotal career decisions early on, and possessing a heart that literally beats to the rhythm of its own drum, are my God-given superpowers— I've used them well and will continue to do so. I'm truly grateful for it all. To be able to enjoy a career that spans over two decades and still be relevant in this business is nothing short of a modern-day miracle; however, I think it's all because my intentions have been pure. I made it my personal mission early on to bless others through music. And all I can say is, what an incredible journey! I hope these chapters have left you inspired as well as motivated to demand more from yourself and from this life. You owe it to you to become the best possible version of yourself, both personally and professionally as well as mentally and spiritually. By crystalizing what my purpose was and fueling that with an unbridled passion, everything that I could imagine I wanted started pursuing me. Not to get too deep but Matthew 6:33 states this, "But more than anything else, put God's work first and do what He wants. Then the other things will be yours as well."

My translation of that scripture is, if you direct all your energy toward ways you can use and amplify what you've been given, your gift— your talent; that thing that you can't stop thinking about, every other need you have will take care of itself. It's like the domino effect. When the first domino falls, it initiates a chain of reaction that knocks down all the other dominos. Through establishing myself in production first, I've launched my own record label, scored films, had starring roles in movies, hosted events, created my own apparel line, founded a clothing store— House of Fresh, been a brand ambassador for several liquor companies, established the Drum Squad Foundation, and conducted the Memphis Symphony Orchestra for my father's retiring performance as he ended his historic career run as the first Black person to hold a first chair clarinetist seat.

That was a surreal moment to honor my dad in that way, especially with him being the one who kept his foot on my neck growing up to learn how to play different instruments. He was there for me during my firsts and I was there for him for his last. It took some time for us to get to that point. My dad wasn't happy with my decision to drop out of college and pursue music as a Hip-Hop producer, but one thing I will say is that you must keep it real with yourself. Hiding how you really feel and trying to make everyone happy doesn't make you nice, it just makes you a liar. That's one of the worst feelings to experience. You're miserable while everybody around you is cool because you're living your life their way. That's when keeping it real goes wrong. You must be at peace with your spirit for things to flow unencumbered into your life in order to receive the fruit from the seeds God planted inside you.

Our brief time on this earth isn't meant to be a struggle. We must let our inner voice guide us and not be distracted by what other people are doing or saying because your dream isn't always meant for other people to understand, if ever. You've got to learn to accept the criticism, the skepticism, and the haters even if they share the same blood as you. Guard your peace of mind and do what brings joy to your soul. Blessed are the peacemakers that have created their own kingdom of heaven.

THANK YOU

I want to thank my parents first and foremost for bringing me into this world and giving me the gift of life. I'm indebted to my mom's side of the family for exposing me to the oldies but goodies; classic songs from the vault of the Stax Records family like Isaac Hayes. They also blessed my ears with the sounds of Al Green, Ann Peebles, Willie Mitchell, and Patti LaBelle as well as friends of the family who had special vocal abilities. My mother also exposed me to church and opera; two distinct influences on my sound. My dad's side exposed me to music theory, music appreciation, and the orchestra.

I'd like to thank my brother for exposing me to hip-hop and introducing me to my first studio experience. I appreciate you bro for giving me the motivation that I needed to take myself to the next level and to take myself and my music production career seriously. You were also the one who put me in the mix of people like Jazze Pha and the whole Noontime family.

Thank you Wendy Day for doing those music business workshops for free in Memphis and taking the time to teach people in the music industry the proper routes to take to copyright music, register records for publishing, the importance of splits sheets, and most importantly, how to make money!

Thank you, Anzel Jennings (aka Redboy). You managed Tela and was the right-hand man of J. Prince and Rap-A-Lot Records. You always handled business and got checks cut for me as well as made sure that my beats got placed including getting me on one of my first albums.

I want to thank Coach K for helping me secure my first platinum plaque through my work with Jeezy.

Chris Hicks, thank you for giving me my first publishing deal at Warner Chappell. The money I got from completing that deal allowed me to prove to my dad that I could make a living doing music.

Thank you William "Squeak" Watkins for not only being my manager but for also believing in me and giving me the opportunity to be heard.

Donald Woodard, you were not just my first attorney, but also a Black attorney who saw my potential as an emerging producer. Thank you for taking a chance on me and accepting me as a client when I didn't have any money.

I want to thank Big Cat Records for opening the door to work with Young Sneed, who I sold the original "Standing Ovation" beat to. It was in Big Cat's studio that I met Gucci Mane.

I want to thank MoneyGraphics for always holding me down with the impeccable artwork and for creating all of my Drum Squad logos, flyers, website and for just keeping my brand fresh.

Jay aka "Listen to this track, bitch." Man, thank you for the tag and staying down with me and believing in me when I first moved to Atlanta.

I've gotta thank Gangsta Boo aka Lola Mitchell, the sister that I never had. You were a ride or die Drumma Boy fan, introducing me to everybody in Atlanta, including Natina Reed from Blaque (R.I.P). Those relationships led me to get placements with Pastor Troy and Boyz N Da Hood. You also had me on your albums when you went solo from Three 6 Mafia, which was a huge blessing.

To Aaron Bay Schuck...you were the A&R at Atlantic Records at the time and we connected through Fiend at S-Line Studios. I played you some beats and you made the Plies and T-Pain song happen and I thank you for that.

Thank you, Downtown Jackson Brown for allowing me to make beats and record out of your studio in Memphis. I was able to meet all the local Memphis rappers and have a home-base to work out of.

To Gary Belz, the owner of House of Blues Studios, thank you for believing in me and giving me a place to work. I made a lot of history there.

DJ Drama, I did my first Gangsta Grillz with you through a group called Blackout Music and I salute you for believing in that project.

THANK YOU

I want to shout out Angie Stone. Thank you for being that Godmama; for always picking up the phone when I needed somebody to talk to, for encouraging me, inspiring me, and motivating me to keep going and to stay positive.

Arthur Sidney, who I met at fourteen-years-old, you've been like another brother to me, even giving me the name Drumma Boy when you first heard my beats. I appreciate you for always being in my corner. You also helped me get my first job at Just For Feet and it changed my life. It put me in the mindset of a salesman, which is how I learned how to sell products, hustle, and understand how to give people what they wanted.

Thank you, Tamiko Hope for helping me bring this vision of writing a book to life and for always being down with me. And you introduced me to Andre 3k and Big Boi. You took me into their offices and told them I was an upcoming producer and somebody they needed to know. Thank you for riding with me and always having good spirits.

Thank you, ASCAP and BMI. I have huge catalogs on both. I want to thank Marché Butler at BMI for helping me register all my records and helping me get my life together at BMI. Anything that I ever needed at BMI, she's always been there. She answers my questions, she hits back, she responds to emails, phone calls, and makes sure the job gets done.

I want to thank Catherine Brewton and the entire BMI team.

Byron Wright, you've done a lot for me and still doing some amazing things today. You've always given me great advice and helped me throughout this creative process, especially navigating this music industry of sharks.

I want to thank Sasha Brookner, my very first publicist. She got me all my early and most significant magazine placements. To Tamara Juda, my current publicist, thank you for the amazing things that we've been able to accomplish on this incredible journey.

Big thank you to the GRAMMYs for recognizing my work, specifically with Usher, Jeezy, Kanye, Plies, 2 Chainz, and T.I. I'm so thankful for being honored by the Recording Academy. I'm Governor of the Memphis GRAMMY chapter as well as a voting member, so it's a pleasure to be aligned with such a prestigious organization.

www.ingramcontent.com/pod-product-compliance
Lightning Source LLC
Chambersburg PA
CBHW042027050526
44107CB00103B/721